Excelling at Dog Agility

Book 2: Sequence Training

Jane Simmons-Moake

Excelling at Dog Agility
Book 2: Sequence Training

Illustrators: Jane Simmons-Moake, Gordon Simmons-Moake, Charles Simmons

Cover Photo: OTCh, ADCh FlashPaws Hollywood Hotshot, UDX, MX, MXJ, BDA-CD, owned by Jane Simmons-Moake. Photo by Bill Newcomb.

Editors: Gordon Simmons-Moake, Susan Roehm, Maggie Downey, Lois Williams

FlashPaws Productions
7714 Rolling Fork Lane
Houston, TX 77040-3432

Library of Congress Catalog Card Number: 00-107395

ISBN 0-9674929-1-2

First Printing, 2000

Printed in the United States of America

Contents

Dogs Appearing in this Book:

- Golden Retrievers *Holly*, OTCh, ADCh, MX, MXJ, UDX, BDA-CD, and *Tracy*, OTCh, ADCh, SKC-Ch, U-CDX, UDX, MX, AXJ, FDCh, JH, WC, VCX, OD, owned by Jane Simmons-Moake

- German Shepherds *Spirit*, OTCh, UDX, ADCh, MX, FDCh, OTD-s, STD-c, STD-d, BDA-CD and *Xena*, MACH, ADCh, MX, MXJ, CDX, owned by Gordon Simmons-Moake

- Border Terrier *Sadie*, MACH, ADCh, CD, MX, MXJ, ME, CG, VE, CGC, owned by Jan Downey

- Golden Retriever *Kelsey*, MACH 2, ADCh, MX, MXJ, CD, EAC, OJC, OGC, RS-E, JS-O, GS-O, CGC, owned by Maggie Downey

- Shetland Sheepdog *Abbey*, MACH, MX, MXJ, owned by Deb Stein

- Border Collie *Partee*, CH, MACH, U-CDX, CDX, MX, MXJ, TD, ASCA-CD, MAD, SM, GM, EAC, EGC, OJC, RS-E, GS-E, JS-O, FMX, CGC, owned by Carol Fatheree

- Golden Retriever *Sunny*, OA, AXJ, NJC, OAC, EGC, JS-N, RS-O, GS-E, CGC, owned by Lois Williams

- Cocker Spaniel *Cody*, MX, MXJ, AAD, RM, JM, SM, OAC, OJC, OGC, RS-O, GS-O, owned by James and Linda Taylor

- Jack Russell Terrier *Action Jackson*, ADCh, MX, MXJ, FDX, CGC, owned by Renee Toth

- Golden Retriever *Tracy*, OA, OAJ, owned by Tom Causey

- Smooth Fox Terrier *Jif*, MX, MXJ, FDCh, GCG, owned by Tom Causey

- Bearded Collie *Jet*, AX, MXJ, AD, NAC, NGC, NJC, RS-N, JS-N, GS-N, owned by Karen Barratt

- Labrador Retriever *Gen*, AX, AXJ, NAC, OJC, OGC, RS-N, JS-O, GS-O, owned by Jackie Bludworth

Special thanks to Janell Copas for appearing in several of the training photographs, and to Tien Tran for allowing us to include some of her wonderful action photography.

Acknowledgments

Sincere thanks to the following people who helped make this book series possible:

- Renee Toth and Jan Downey, for always being there and for keeping FlashPaws on track while I worked to finish this project.

- Gordon Simmons-Moake, Susan Roehm, Maggie Downey, and Lois Williams, for their expert help in reviewing the manuscript.

- Charles Simmons and Gordon Simmons-Moake, for their superb illustrations.

- Our wonderful students and their dogs, who make it all worthwhile by providing continuous support and inspiration.

The author and Holly, OTCh, ADCh, FlashPaws Hollywood Hotshot UDX, MX, MXJ, BDA-CD

About Book 2

Welcome to *Book 2: Sequence Training* — the second in a three-volume set entitled *Excelling at Dog Agility*. Whether you are totally new to the sport or are a seasoned veteran, it is highly recommended that you first master the skills in *Book 1: Obstacle Training*, before progressing to *Book 2*. Within its pages you will find essential foundation principles for guiding all of your future agility training.

Book 2 will guide you on a step-by-step path to achieving the ultimate in teamwork with your dog. You will learn to sequence smoothly and efficiently from one obstacle to the next through turns and winding pathways. The resulting skills will help you reach your dog's highest potential for speed and accuracy in the competition ring.

The topics and exercises in the three books of this series correspond with three tapes of the award-winning video series entitled *Competitive Agility Training with Jane Simmons-Moake*. This book corresponds to *Tape 2: Sequence Training*. You may find it helpful to refer to the exercises on the video tapes. Seeing the exercises demonstrated can add an extra dimension to the text and illustrations presented in this book.

You can find more information about the *Competitive Agility Training* video series at the back of this book.

Sit!, Down!, Stay!, and Come! are basic obedience commands that are absolutely vital to your success in the agility ring.

1 Obedience, Directional, and Control Commands

If you have followed the training procedures in *Book 1: Obstacle Training*, you have mastered each of the competition obstacles to the highest of standards. Now it is time to begin chaining the obstacles together in smooth-flowing sequences.

Obedience, directional, and control commands are the tools you will use — along with your obstacle commands, signals, and body cues — to guide your dog through the agility course. Before starting any sequencing, your dog must have reliable responses to certain essential obedience commands. It will also be to your advantage to begin training some of the directional and control commands you will be using.

Essential Obedience Commands

Sit!, Down!, Stay!, and *Come!* are basic obedience commands that are **absolutely vital** to your success in the agility ring. The responses to all of these commands must be immediate and unequivocal. For some dogs, training these four commands alone can constitute a considerable challenge. The upside to this, however, is that once you have achieved your goal, you will be rewarded with a dog that is a joy to live with, and can happily (and safely) accompany you in many of your travels. In agility, the obedience commands are used as follows:

Sit

You will need the *Sit!* command for leaving your dog at the start line or at the beginning of an exercise. It can also be a required position on the pause table in agility competition. A lightning-fast response to the *Sit!* command will help reduce your time spent on the course and result in more competitive scores.

Down (or Drop)

A fast response to the *Down!* command is also vital when the down position is required on the pause table. Many handlers lose time on the table as a result of a slow response to the *Down!* command. If you have repeatedly used this command in your household activities and have accepted slow responses, you may want to retrain a new command, such as *Drop!*, which requires a speedy response. Henceforth, any time you ask your dog to *Drop!* he must do so quickly to meet your criteria for success.

Stay (or Wait)

A reliable response to the *Stay!* or *Wait!* command is required for keeping your dog at the start line or table, or at the beginning of a training exercise while you lead out.

Some handlers use *Stay!* and *Wait!* to mean different things – especially those who participate in competitive obedience. In these cases, often *Stay!* means "remain in place until I return to release you. Attention is not required." *Wait!* means "remain in position with full attention until I give you your next command." If you use this distinction between these two commands, then *Wait!* is more appropriate for your agility training.

Come (or Here)

Of all the obedience commands, the *Come!* command, or **recall**, is paramount to your success in the agility ring. You will use the command to turn the dog quickly in your direction and to call him off incorrect obstacles in his path.

Some people prefer to use an alternative command such as *Here!*, because they worry that using *Come!* might interfere with their dog's training for the obedience ring. We have been using *Come!* in the agility ring for years — even with our obedience champions — and we have never seen it negatively affect competitive obedience work. If you prefer, however, using a command such as *Here!* is perfectly acceptable. In fact, you could call your recall command *Cabbage!* if you wanted to. Regardless of what command you use, you **must** train the command thoroughly and systematically to mean *"the dog must come quickly and immediately on your first and only command, without taking side trips and without succumbing to distractions."*

If you fail to require an immediate response in training, you cannot expect one in the agility ring. You will have chosen instead the ulcer-causing handling strategy of "cross-your-fingers-and pray." By the time you've uttered your third *Here!*, it will most likely be too late to prevent your dog from incurring a fault.

Correction-Free Training

Is it possible to train without ever using corrections? Yes, it can be done. Correction-free training may be your only option with ultra-sensitive dogs or fearful rescue dogs that may have come from abusive backgrounds. For the vast majority of other dogs, however, choosing to train correction-free means you must be willing to accept the consequences. Unless you are blessed with a one-in-a-million dog that has an overwhelming desire to please you over pleasing himself, you will likely have performances that are erratic and unpredictable. Most dogs trained correction-free will work with you as long as the promise of a reward from you is more reinforcing than any other stimulus that is also available. If your dog really enjoys sniffing interesting scents or making up his own course, he may well decide these activities are more self-fulfilling than the promise of any reward you may have to offer.

If, despite this warning, correction-free training is the road you choose, you will get the most reliable performances if you work hard to make your reward schedule unpredictable. If the dog never knows what reward he is trading the behavior for he will be more likely to remain working with you in hopes of receiving a jackpot. It will also help to convince the dog that he might be rewarded in the agility ring at any time. To achieve this end, attend as many fun matches and show-and-gos as possible and reward your dog lavishly in the ring at unpredictable moments.

Training With Corrections

An alternative to a correction-free approach is a common-sense approach incorporating both positive and negative. This training philosophy usually produces a more reliable and happy working dog. It also promotes a better dog/handler working relationship — one in which the dog eagerly accepts the handler as leader. Since you, the handler, are the only team member who can read the numbers on the course, it is a definite advantage to have sealed your position as leader of your dog/handler team.

Using this commonsense approach, all initial training on every desired behavior is totally positive. Training focuses on slowly and systematically showing the dog what you want and helping him to be right. After the dog understands thoroughly what you want, the dog is gradually presented with enticing alternatives. At some point, the dog will feel he has a choice about whether to investigate the distraction or comply with your command. When this occurs, a well-timed, fair, and appropriate correction helps communicate to your dog that the alternative behavior is unacceptable — just as a mother wolf would discipline her cub when his behavior got out of line.

When applying corrections, keep the following in mind:

- **Use only the smallest correction needed** to cause a change in behavior on subsequent tries. Sometimes a verbal correction is all a dog needs. If your dog repeats his error, however, your correction was not strong enough or was not well-timed.

- **Use a few significant corrections** rather than frequent, small, nagging ones.

- **Never allow yourself to become angry** during training. Anger is counterproductive in achieving your training goals. Your dog has a right to test the limits of what you will accept. You have a right to insist that he do it your way.

- **Follow** physical corrections, which force the dog to perform the desired behavior, **with immediate praise** — even though your correction helped him to comply.

- Follow both physical and verbal corrections with an **immediate opportunity to try again**. After a correction, reward generously at the first sign of success.

- If you are the least bit unsure whether a mistake was yours or your dog's **always give the dog the benefit of the doubt and forego the correction**. Training with a friend can give you immediate feedback about who caused the error.

Training the Obedience Commands

This book does not cover procedures for training your dog to sit, stay, down, and come on command. You can find instructions in any one of many excellent obedience training books found in bookstores or libraries. Better yet, enroll in an obedience class. You will enjoy the benefits of expert feedback and guidance, while gaining the opportunity to train among the distractions of other dogs and people.

Regarding your obedience training, however, consider the following advice:

- **Set your standards high.** With hard work and ingenuity, every dog can be trained to perform a snappy sit, down, and come; and a rock-solid stay. You do not have to settle for slow or unreliable responses!

- **Teach your basic obedience commands away from the time and place you train agility.** To achieve swift and reliable responses to your obedience commands, it likely that you will need to administer a few corrections. Corrections done properly are well-timed, fair, unemotional, and suited to the dog's temperament. Trainers who make proper and careful use of corrections have dogs that maintain a very positive attitude toward their training and their handlers. Nevertheless, no matter how earnestly you try to be fair, it is easy to slip up occasionally and correct a dog unfairly. To prevent any possible negative transfer of attitude to your dog's agility work, keep your essential obedience command training separate from your agility work.

- **Proof for distractions.** Don't consider your obedience commands trained until the dog is reliable when faced with a variety of visual, audible, and scent distractions. Once your dog has thoroughly learned his commands in a distraction-free environment, gradually add distractions until the dog is reliable in a wide variety of situations. This includes never allowing the dog to sniff while under a command. (He can sniff all he likes when off-duty.) If you work through this common problem in your obedience work, you should not encounter a sniffing problem in your agility training.

- **Monitor and maintain.** Once you have trained, proofed, and are using the obedience commands in your agility training, be alert to any weakening of the commands. Like all other training, your obedience commands will require periodic maintenance to keep them sharp and reliable.

Directional and Control Commands

Besides the essential obedience commands there are additional directional and control commands you will want to train.

Out

One of the most useful commands in agility is the *Out!* command. It means *"turn away from the handler."* For example, if handling your dog off the left, (i.e., you are to the right of the dog) *Out!* signals a turn to the left. (Figure 1-1.) Its opposite command, *Come!* or *Here!*, is used to mean *"turn toward the handler."*

> **NOTE:** *In Figure 1-1 and in all of the illustrations to follow, "D" represents the dog, and "H" represents the handler.*

There are many ways to train *Out!*; however, the method described in this book requires sequencing skills. Therefore, the procedures are described in *Chapter 6: Training the Out! command.*

A WORD ABOUT *LEFT!* AND *RIGHT!*

Some handlers choose to use *Left!* and *Right!* commands to direct their dogs to turn to the left or right. These commands refer to the dog's left and right and are independent of the handler's position.

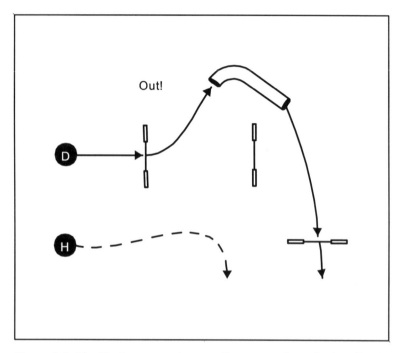

Figure 1-1: The Out! command means "turn away from the handler."

In an ideal world, all dogs would learn to reliably respond to the *Right!* and *Left!* commands, regardless of the position of the handler. In reality this is a very difficult goal. Most handlers who believe their dogs understand the commands for left and right have dogs that are responding only to body cues. The handler could say *Godzilla!* instead of *Right!* and the dog would turn in the correct direction. There are times, however, that it would be advantageous to have a dog that truly understood *Left!* and *Right!.*

First, you need to decide if it is worth it to you to attempt to train these commands. If you have a dog that is highly verbal, and you have an abundance of time on your hands, it might be worth it. The majority of dogs, however are not highly verbal. They have difficulty ignoring body cues in favor of verbal directions. Thus, it takes quite a bit of time to teach and almost as much effort to maintain the *Left!* and

Right! commands. Keep in mind, also, that even with a dog that fully understands these directional commands, the handler must give the correct command at the appropriate time. Since *Left!* and *Right* refer to the dog's left and right, the handler may require a fraction of a second to determine the correct command to say. This often results in late commands.

Using *Come!* and *Out!* for directional control can effectively cover your directional needs in all of your course work. Moreover, it is a more practical alternative to teaching the more elusive concepts of *Left!* and *Right!* A big advantage is that *Come!* and *Out!* are more intuitive for most handlers. As a result, it is easier for the handler to give a well-timed command for the correct direction — especially when the unexpected happens or when the handler is under the stress of competition. Another advantage is that these commands are faster and easier for the dog to learn, especially for dogs who do not possess exceptional verbal aptitude.

Line Up

Line up! is a command that means *"move swiftly to my left side in a sit-at-heel position and wait for further instructions."* This command allows you to quickly set up your dog in position at the start line or at the beginning of an exercise during training. Without a *Line up!* command, handlers waste precious training time trying to get their dogs into position, focused, and ready to work. Because it is time-consuming to position your dog through repeated approximations, your dog is likely to become bored and inattentive during the process. He may also lose attitude as a result of the physical manhandling and the tedious begging required to place a poorly trained dog in a precise and advantageous start position.

Line up! can be taught anywhere, anytime, without access to agility obstacles. Thus, the Line up! command is perfect for training at home during a spare moment, or on days when the weather prevents you from venturing outside to train.

Line up! can be taught anywhere, anytime, without access to agility obstacles.

To train the *Line up!* command, begin with your dog in a position facing you and to the left of you. Place a treat or toy — whichever your dog likes the most — in your left hand. Command *Line up!* (or whatever you decide to call your command) and take a step back with your left foot, leaving your right foot in its original position. At the same time bring the hand with your incentive close to the dog's nose and then out and back behind you as you step back.

When your dog aligns himself with your left leg, return your left foot to a position in line with your right foot. As the dog follows, command him to *Sit!* when he reaches approximate heel position (at your left side facing the direction that you are facing) and raise the incentive over his head. When he sits in the desired position, release him with a command to *Get It!* and drop the treat or toy to your dog's mouth for him to catch. Gradually decrease the step backwards until the dog will move to the correct position without your stepping back at all. You will also want to vary the dog's starting position until he can line up from any location.

Once your dog understands what *Line up!* means, you can begin requiring that the dog line up more quickly. Make it a fun game. Get the dog excited by running around with him and then suddenly give your command to *Line up!* If he complies reasonably well, praise and release with a command to *Get it!* and drop the treat or toy in his mouth. From this point, gradually increase your standards, requiring a faster response to earn a reward.

> **NOTE:** *Training Line up! is similar to training a swing finish, for those who train for obedience competition. If you have already trained a swing finish for obedience, you may choose to use the same command for lining up in agility. Be aware, however, that if you choose this option, you must expect the same degree of precision in agility (sitting straight, in perfect heel position, etc.) that you expect in the obedience ring. If you would rather not demand this level of precision, use a different command to line up in agility and train it separately.*

Again

Again! is a command that means *"take the obstacle you just performed in the opposite direction."* It is not a directional command per se but an obstacle command. The beauty of the *Again!* command is that its meaning remains exactly the same regardless of the handler's position on the course.

Although it has very little use on a Standard or Jumpers course, the *Again!* command is useful for accumulating points quickly in Gamblers competition. It is even more valuable while training for teaching the dog to listen closely and pay attention to your commands and signals. Once you have patterned your dog to perform a sequence, you can surprise him with changes of direction and random *Agains!* to keep him on his toes and listening to you. These games of variations on a theme are fun for the dog and keep training interesting for both of you. Ideally, it will be to your advantage to teach the dog to *Again!* on all of the obstacles that are bi-directional. The easiest way to start teaching this command is with an open tunnel.

Arrange the tunnel in an arc. With the dog on your left side, command and signal the dog to the left end of the tunnel. As he exits, command *Again!* and step in with your right foot, signaling a return through the tunnel with your right hand. (If necessary, repeat the *Tunnel!* command. Eliminate the command for the tunnel, however, as soon as possible. There may be confusion as to whether you want the dog to take the tunnel in the opposite direction or whether you want him to take the first end of the tunnel he sees.)

To eliminate any ambiguity, be careful to use the proper body position, facing the path you want the dog to take (Figure 1-2 – left panel). Over-turning by facing the obstacle itself can cause ambiguity as to which side of the tunnel you want the dog to enter (Figure 1-2 – right panel).

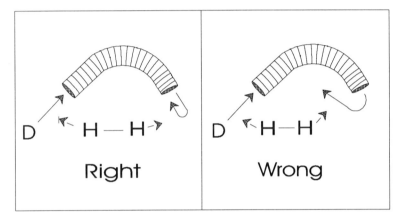

Figure 1-2: Training the Again! command.

Progress by increasing your distance from the dog, then by gradually eliminating your signal and body movements until the dog can perform an *Again!* on a verbal command alone. Although you will be able to use a signal as well as a verbal in the competition ring, teaching the dog to respond to the verbal alone gives you extra insurance when the dog is working at a great distance.

Train the *Again!* command next on the jumps and the tire. Then train it on the A-frame, dog walk, and weave poles.

Straight

Straight! means *"run in a straight line until I ask you to do something else."* *Straight!* refers to the point of view of the dog, not the handler. This command is similar to the obedience go-out and is useful for sending your dog across the finish line. It also is handy for the occasional times when the dog is not close enough to the next obstacle to be able to focus on it well. *Straight!* can also be used when you want to send the dog out to approach a distant obstacle from the opposite side.

You can train *Straight!* in any of the ways used to train the obedience go-out. If you are currently competing in obedience or plan to in the future, it is best to use a different command for the go-out than the one you use for *Straight!*, and to train the commands separately. This will help prevent confusion or any likelihood that your Utility dog will decide to take one of the jumps on his way out to the go-out spot.

One way to train *Straight!* is to use a target and a barrier, followed by the addition of obstacles. This procedure is described in *Book 3: Advanced Skills Training*.

A WORD ABOUT *"GO!"*

Although *Go!* is a perfectly acceptable command word to use in place of either of the precisely-defined *Out!* or *Straight!* commands, most handlers do not use it as such. No word on the agility course is as commonly misused as the *Go!* command. You will often hear handlers prefacing most of their obstacle commands with *Go!* while in the agility ring. For example, *Go tunnel!, Go dog walk!, Go weave!* When asked to define what their *Go!* command means, many handlers are often at a loss. Some respond with, *"You know... Go! Go away from me!"* There are many possible directions away from the handler — 360 degrees worth! Which do you want your dog to choose? That description of *Go!* is far too vague for your dog to understand. If you can't define the performance you are looking for, how can your dog ever be right or wrong? Does the *Go!* command have anything to do with the dog's current path? Does it refer in any way to the handler's body position?

Your obstacle commands should completely and more precisely cover what you are trying to accomplish with *Go! The command Dog Walk!* means *"find the dog walk and get on squarely." The command Jump!* or *Over!* means *"take the jump you are looking at."* The *Go!* command is not only unnecessary — it takes extra time and gives no useful information to the dog.

When handlers use the *Go!* command, it delays the important obstacle or directional command that follows it. At the point at which the dog must make a decision between two adjacent obstacles, such as when in mid-air over a jump, the dog decides on the correct next obstacle on the basis of hearing *Go!*, which is non-specific as far as an obstacle or direction is concerned. The dog could easily second-guess that you want him to go to the tunnel on the basis of hearing *Go!*, rather than the adjacent jump you wanted him to take.

As long as the next obstacle is within reasonable viewing distance for the dog, such as within 25 feet or so, you should expect your dog to take it on a well-timed obstacle command, regardless of whether you are running with the dog or not. If you have not trained your dog to run out ahead of you at full speed to each of the obstacles at a variety of angles and distances, review the procedures in *Book 1: Obstacle Training*.

For obstacles that you consider too far away for your dog to see (which is a rare occurrence), you can use your *Straight!* command to send the dog in a straight line until he can see the correct obstacle. Then give your obstacle command.

You are ready to begin sequencing when your dog has fully mastered each of the obstacles. (Photo: Tien Tran Photography)

2 Sequencing for Success

You are ready to begin your sequence training when — and ONLY when — your dog can:

- **Perform each of the obstacles confidently and quickly on your first and only command, from a variety of angles and distances.** A good rule of thumb is if your dog isn't solid on an obstacle don't include it in a sequence.

- **Perform an off-lead sit, stay, down, and come on your first and only command, quickly and reliably, with all types of distractions present.** If you begin sequencing without these important obedience skills, your dog is likely to develop unwanted habits that can be very difficult to correct. Such habits might include breaking stays at the start line or at the pause table, spinning, sniffing, barking, head checking, running out of the ring, turning back to the handler after one or more obstacles, running past obstacles, or taking the wrong obstacle.

Many people get hooked on agility and start sequencing much too early in their training. They become so excited about progressing in the sport and entering their first agility trial that they begin sequencing before many of the essential obstacle-training and obedience prerequisites have been satisfied. Unfortunately, the negative habits formed through premature or careless sequence training will most likely remain with the dog to some degree throughout his agility career.

You will be much more satisfied with your ring performances if you take a patient and systematic approach to sequencing, while keeping some important principles in mind.

Sequencing Principles

The following guidelines should apply to all of your sequence training:

- **Start short and simple. Strive for short stretches of excellence** rather than long stretches of mediocrity. Performing a smooth three-obstacle sequence is much better than performing a crunchy five-obstacle sequence.

- **Set your standards high.** Stop immediately and address problems the moment they occur. In particular, you should never accept spinning, barking, sniffing, head checks, lack of enthusiasm or speed, attention lapses, inaccurate obstacle performance, or refusals.

  It is especially important not to accept refusals, as they waste time and often result in penalties. Unfortunately, it is easy to accidentally teach a dog that refusals are acceptable. Have you ever seen this training scenario? A handler is attempting to send his dog over a jump and to a pause table without the handler going past the jump. The handler commands *Over!* and *Table!* Instead of going to the table the dog turns back to the handler as if to say "Do what, now?, Did you say table?" The handler gets increasingly agitated, repeating *"Go table! Go table!"* Eventually the dog heads to the table and jumps on. The dog is rewarded.

  What's wrong with this situation? The dog has been rewarded for checking back and not continuing smoothly to the table. As a result, the dog may develop this behavior as a crutch. You can avoid this problem by setting your standards for excellence from the start and never accepting refusals in training. When faced with a refusal, stop, then make it easier to succeed on the next try. Reward generously for successfully executing the behavior you had in mind.

- **Work with a partner** to help provide feedback. Concentrate on your timing of commands and your consistency of signals and body language. If your timing needs improvement, have your partner give well-timed commands at the same time that you are commanding your dog through a sequence. If your voice sounds like an echo of your friend's, you know your commands are late.

- When the goal of an exercise is **to teach a new sequencing maneuver, use only low, single jumps.** While learning a sequencing skill, you don't want the dog to worry about jumping a challenging height or spread. Moreover, you don't want the dog to displace any bars. If he does, you will need to interrupt your sequence training to address the problem. Once you've perfected the skill at a low height, you can gradually raise the jump heights and add spread jumps.

- Remember to work sequences **off the right as frequently as you work them off the left**. Doing so will prevent both you and the dog from developing a preference for one side or the other.

- Normal spacing between obstacles in an agility ring is 18 –20 feet, with a minimum of 21 feet before and after spread jumps such as the double-bar jump, the triple-bar jump, and the broad jump. When you first begin your sequence training, **start with the obstacles spaced about 16-18 feet apart.** This will make it easier for your dog to smoothly focus from one obstacle to the next. (You will not be using spread jumps in your early sequence training.) Once your dog has caught on to the concept of sequencing, you can space the obstacles as they would normally be spaced at an agility trial. Once your dog is more experienced, you will also want to practice occasionally with the obstacles spaced 25 – 30 feet apart. This will help prepare you for times when the obstacles are spaced wider apart than usual.

Sequence Training Tools

For sequence training, you will need an abundant supply of treats and/or toys. If using food, soft, highly palatable treats work best. Avoid crunchy or overly large training treats. For best results, the pieces should be small enough to be eaten quickly, but large enough to be worth working for. If you have a hard-to-motivate dog, make sure your treats are ex-tra-special and train only when your dog is hungry. You may even want to give your dog his meals during your train-ing sessions.

You will also need a tight-fitting buckle collar and a short, knot-ted **grab tab**. This combination will give you a handle to launch or direct your dog when neces-sary.

Don't use a leash while se-quencing. If you are worried that you will need a leash, perhaps you don't trust your dog's *Stay!* or *Come!* com-mands. Or, perhaps you don't trust your dog's performance on each of the individual obstacles? If this is the case, it would be a good idea to postpone your sequence training until your foundation training is more reliable.

Using a leash for sequencing can be problematic in several ways:

- **It can be dangerous.** If the dog is moving at a good rate of speed (which you want to encourage!), you can easily get the leash caught on an obstacle. This can cause your dog to lose confidence, which could make him reluctant to jump on subsequent attempts. It could even result in an injury to you or your dog.

- Using a leash **encourages the dog to slow down** and take shorter strides to match your pace. It also patterns the dog to **work closely** alongside you. When you decide later that you want the dog to run faster or work at a distance, you are likely to experience resistance, resulting in the need to retrain.

- Using a leash on a jump sequence can restrict the dog's natural movements. This can **negatively effect the dog's jumping style** to the point where it creates poor jumping habits.

Besides rewards, an appropriate collar, and a tab, there are other training aids you may want to use. All are intended to help the dog be successful without the use of a leash or other physical manhandling. Your dog will learn more quickly and will have a better attitude toward training if you teach him to actively respond to your cues on his own, rather than by forcing him. What's more, he will learn from the start to work on his own in response to your commands and body cues. This is important since in the competition ring, you will need to communicate your wishes without using physical contact.

The following are several other tools that you may find useful in your sequence training:

Targets to help the dog be correct and to encourage him to work away from you

Wire guides or other devices to channel the dog in the desired direction

Objects to throw to encourage the dog to work ahead of the handler in a specific direction, such as toys, balls, or food containers with scent holes

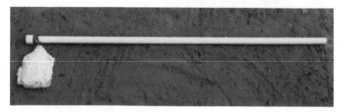

A luring device such as a **toy-on-a-stick** for dogs that need encouragement to focus ahead on a sequence

Developing a Consistent Set of Cues

In the competition ring, your success will largely depend on how well you communicate to your dog where to go. Simply put, sequence training is a matter of teaching your dog "when I do this, you do that."

Consider what it would be like working with a human dance partner. In your practice sessions, you and your partner would need to work on training and polishing the individual parts of your dance routine (skill training) and developing a set of agreed-upon cues that signify "when I do this, you do that" (teamwork training). This is exactly what you will be doing when you train your dog to excel in agility.

The actual cues you choose to communicate with your dog are not as important as the fact that they are clear, consistent, and unambiguous. If your cues meet these criteria, your dog will have little or no uncertainty about where you want him to go. The result will be fast, smooth, and confident agility runs.

Your consistent set of cues comprises a combination of verbal commands, hand signals, and body language.

Verbal Commands

Your dog will have the best chance for smooth sequencing if your verbal commands are well-timed. Your dog needs to know where to go next before he completes the previous obstacle.

When the previous obstacle is a jump, you should give your command no later than when the dog is directly above the bar. Any later and the dog's head will most likely start to turn back to you. If this happens, he will lose time and be more likely to incur a fault on the next obstacle (such as a runout or a knocked bar). For extremely fast dogs, give your command for the next obstacle as the dog leaves the ground for the jump.

Your voice commands should be pleasant, clear, confident, and enthusiastic. Your tone should be interesting, not monotone. All praise should sound sincere, not robot-like or gratuitous. Dogs tend to tune out handlers who use a relentlessly high-pitched, chirpy (or begging) tone of voice. Likewise, they will lose attitude if you bellow your commands like an army sergeant. Overly harsh commands may also be penalized in the agility ring. Enunciate your commands clearly — don't mumble! The more confident you sound, the more your dog will have confidence in you as a team leader.

If you have a dog that is either extremely excitable or very easy-going, you may benefit from adjusting your tone of voice to suit your dog's temperament. The more excitable or frantic your dog is, the calmer and more controlled your voice will need to be. Conversely, to get the most out of a slower, more tentative dog, you will need to inject a generous amount of enthusiasm and excitement in your commands and praise.

All of the commands you use in the agility ring should have a well-defined, mutually understood meaning. Don't issue commands you have not trained. You are likely to lose your dog's trust in you as a team leader.

When sequencing, it is a good idea to eliminate all extraneous talking or chatter. When your important commands are buried in a sea of meaningless chatter, it can be difficult for your dog to process what you are trying to communicate. Because so much of your talking is inconsequential, your dog may easily learn to tune you out.

When you keep your handling clean and free of nonessential talking, your dog can more easily focus on what's important. This means using only one command per obstacle and refraining from using your dog's name or praise between obstacles. Doing so will help prevent your dog from looking back to you, which can cause a slow or choppy performance. Moreover, it will help you deliver your next command in a timely fashion.

Signals

A clear, consistent signal is essential for directing your dog along the path you want him to take. Keep in mind the following when giving signals:

- **Use a flat-hand signal** — never a pointed finger. A flat hand is much easier for your dog to see.

- For consistency and visibility, always **use the hand closest to the dog**. Using the opposite hand makes your signal less visible. What's more, it may cause your shoulder to turn suddenly toward your dog, inadvertently signaling him to turn away from you. Using the opposite hand may also cause you to encroach upon your dog's path, pushing him out of the correct line for the next obstacle.

- Your signal should **deliberately and smoothly place the dog along your chosen path**. Your hand need not be extended continuously; however, to communicate clearly with your dog, it should be visible for more than a brief instant. Just as important, the release of your signal should be smooth and controlled. Dropping or retracting your signaling hand wildly or suddenly can call attention to you, the handler, and cause an interruption in your dog's forward movement.

- **Your signal should be steady** relative to the forward movement of your body. Giving a sweeping signal, i.e., where your signaling arm moves in an arc while your body does not move, gives conflicting signals that may pull your dog off of the intended path.

- Giving your signal while the dog is in a stay position at the start line or table can give you the competitive advantage of advance communication about the correct upcoming sequence. To fully exploit this advantage, be sure to proof your dog against breaking his stay on your body movements or signals. He must wait until released with a verbal command for the next obstacle.

For clear and consistent communication, give a flat-hand signal using the hand closest to the dog.

Body Language

Paramount to your success in communicating with your dog is your body language. Dogs communicate with each other primarily using body language, so it's not surprising that body cues carry the greatest weight in communicating with your dog. In agility, your body language communicates most clearly to the dog where you want him to go. When you give verbal commands that conflict with your body language, most dogs will follow your body language. You will discover this the first time you command *Tunnel!* or issue some other incorrect command while directing your dog to the tire jump with your body. Most dogs will not hesitate to perform the tire jump. In another example, you might command your dog to *Come!* but your body bends forward and pushes ahead, telling your dog to take the tunnel in front of him. Guess where the dog will go!

Many people naturally assume that facing the obstacle you want the dog to take would be the obvious body cue to communicate where to go. In reality, this is not the case. When you look at your body language from the dog's vantage point, facing the obstacle often causes uncertainty which can result in slow or incorrect responses from the dog. This is particularly true when you are working at a distance from your dog.

It is your job as a handler to direct the dog to take a path that smoothly and efficiently leads him through the proper sequence of obstacles. You will get the best results if you face your body — including feet, pelvis, and shoulders — toward the path (the line on the ground) you want the dog to take. This concept was illustrated several times in *Book 1: Obstacle Training* and will be illustrated again throughout the sequencing exercises in this book.

It is also important to keep your body moving. When you stop moving, you cease giving your dog information about where you want him to go. Your dog may stop or slow down, or he may continue ahead on a path of his choosing. Making sure your body continues to move on the course requires planning on your part. If you run up quickly to an obstacle and get there before your dog does, you may run out of room to keep moving. This may cause one of the reactions mentioned above, or you may feel the need to start moving ahead or pulling away before your dog is committed to the correct obstacle. Either could result in faults in competition.

Whenever your dog makes a mistake in your training sessions, freeze and look down at your feet. Your feet are usually a good indicator of where your body language is directing the dog. They should be facing the desired path — about midway between where your dog was and the obstacle you wanted him to take. If that's not where you were facing, you know who is to blame!

Using winged jumps encourages your dog to work confidently at a moderate distance from you.

<u>3</u> Straight-Line Sequences

When the next obstacle to take is directly in line with your dog's vision and path, we call it a **straight-line sequence**. These sequences require no turns, so they are the best with which to begin your sequence training.

Jump Sequences

Although it can be easier to begin your sequence training using wingless jumps, it can be beneficial to start with winged jumps instead. Doing so prevents you from developing an early habit of running too closely alongside your dog. What's more, it requires you to think about your body language and handling path from the very first time you begin to sequence. Even more important, using winged jumps encourages your dog to work confidently at a moderate distance from you.

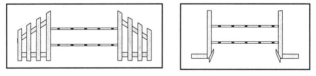

Figure 3-1: Winged (left) and wingless (right) single jumps.

How to Begin

Set up a sequence of three jumps (Figure 3-2) with the bars set low. Start with a two-jump sequence using only jumps

#2 and #3. Leave your dog behind jump #2 and lead out to a position outside the wing of jump #3 (H1). Keep your left shoulder turned slightly inward toward the dog.

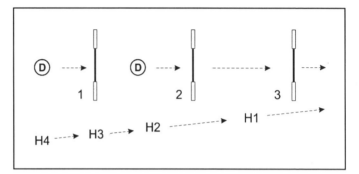

Figure 3-2: Straight-line sequence with jumps.

Make sure you have your dog's attention before beginning. Without using his name, a release word, or *Come!,* command and signal him over jump #2, then immediately move forward. Give your command for jump #3 no later than when the dog is in mid-air over the bar of jump #2. If you give it any later, your dog's head may start to turn and he will no longer be looking at the next obstacle.

If all goes well, progress to three jumps, leading out between jumps #1 and #2 (handler position H2). Each time you are successful, gradually reduce the amount of lead-out (H3), starting in a progressively wider position from the jumps as you do. Keep reducing your lead-out until you are starting even with your dog (H4). By starting wider from the jumps, you can take a slightly converging path, which will help your dog find the sequence.

Be sure to work the exercise off both your right and your left.

When sequencing with jumps, give your next command no later than the moment your dog's head is mid-air over the bar. (Photo: Pat Vandecapelle)

> **TRAINING TIP:** Never use the dog's name or praise in the middle of a straight-line sequence. This will draw his attention to you rather than to the upcoming obstacle, which may cause him to slow down, knock a bar, or bypass the next obstacle.

If You Have Problems...

BROKEN STAYS

...Your dog may have **broken his stay**. Allowing him to do so and then continuing will only teach him that he can decide when to start To get an advantageous head start on your dog, you will need to be able to move quickly and freely at the start line and at the pause table without releasing him from his stay.

- If your dog breaks his stay, give an immediate verbal correction to mark the point of error and place him back in position. Repeat your *Stay!* or *Wait!* command

and lead out two or three steps. If your dog remains in position, quickly return to him and quietly praise and reward him while he remains in position. If he breaks his stay in anticipation of the reward, use your verbal correction and withdraw the food. Then praise when the dog has reassumed his position.

- On subsequent attempts, gradually increase your lead-out distance from the dog while making your motions faster and more dramatic. Return and reward for the desired behavior. Correct any and all attempts to break the stay. After a mistake, make it easier to succeed on the next try, then slowly raise the criteria until your dog will stay under any condition he may encounter — and then some.

To prevent mistakes at the beginning of a sequence, use only the obstacle command to release the dog from his stay — don't preface it with his name, a *Come!* command, or a release word. If you do, your dog may start moving and make an incorrect choice before hearing your obstacle command.

If you have already trained him to hold his position until he hears his name or a release word, you can easily retrain him to follow your new rules by doing the following:

- Find an incentive to throw such as a toy or food container.

- Have a friend excite and restrain your dog as you lead out to the other side of the jump.

- Show the dog the toy, command him to jump (without prefacing it with his name, a release word or a *Come!* command) and immediately throw the toy. The combination of the excited restraint and the thrown reward will help ensure that your dog takes the jump on your first and only *Jump!* command.

- Gradually wean the dog off the restraint. Then, keep the toy hidden and throw it only intermittently as a reward (rather than as a lure) after the dog has committed to the jump.

- After your dog has thoroughly learned your new rules, you should expect him to jump on your first and only command. If he doesn't, follow through with a motivational pop toward the jump using his tab. Follow with lavish praise and an opportunity to try again.

> *TRAINING TIP: As always, when releasing the dog to a toy or a target, use a release command such as Get it!. This release is important because you do not want to allow your dog to think that he is permitted to check out items of interest while he is working with you on the course. He must wait until he has been released by you. This will become even more important when you begin placing distractions on the course for him to ignore.*

LATE COMMANDS

...Your dog may have **failed to continue ahead smoothly with the sequence**. For example, he may have bypassed an obstacle, hesitated before an obstacle, checked back to look at you for direction, or spun in a circle in front of an obstacle. This could easily be caused by **your commands being late.** For your dog to be able to smoothly proceed from one obstacle to the next, you must give your command for the next obstacle before he completes the current obstacle. When sequencing with jumps this means no later than when your dog's head is in mid-air over the bar. Any later and your dog is likely to turn his head back toward you, which contributes to a "crunchy" or choppy sequence.

To determine whether this was your problem, repeat the sequence while having a friend give well-timed commands from the sidelines. If your voice sounds like an echo of your friend's, your commands are late.

If late commands are a recurring problem, it will help you to continue to work with a partner for all of your sequence training to provide you with continuous feedback. When you no longer hear an echo, you know your commands are on time.

It's important to clear up any problems with command timing early in your sequence training. If you train for a considerable length of time giving late commands, your dog will see the arrangement as this: "I take an obstacle and my Mom tells me what I just took." Changing the rules farther down the line can cause confusion, a lack of trust in your leadership, and a definite need for retraining.

Late commands are very common and can be extremely detrimental to reaching your goal of smooth agility excellence. Take heart, however! It's likely that once you have trained yourself to give timely commands, it will become perfectly natural to you and you will do it automatically throughout all of your agility training and competing, without even being consciously aware of it. The key to success is to remedy the problem very early in your sequence training, so that bad habits never become business-as-usual for you or your dog.

INAPPROPRIATE BODY LANGUAGE

Besides late commands, another reason your dog may hesitate, spin, or bypass an obstacle is that you could have pulled him off with **inappropriate body language.**

Make sure you begin far enough laterally away from the dog and converge slightly inward as he completes the sequence. Remaining outside a line made by the wings allows you to continue in a smooth, slightly converging path.

If your path takes you inside the wings you will eventually be forced to pull out, most likely taking your dog with you (Figure 3-3).

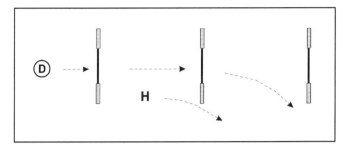

Figure 3-3: A diverging handling path causes a runout.

LACK OF CONFIDENCE

…Your dog may **have refused to continue ahead despite your good handling**. This may be due to a lack of experience and confidence on the part of your dog.

To help him be successful, try one of the following:

- Throw a toy or food container over the last jump as you give your last command to jump. If you have trouble throwing the incentive accurately between the jump wings, have a friend throw it from the opposite side of the jump.

- Place a treat on a target at the end of the sequence and show it to your dog before beginning. Have a friend ready to cover the target to keep your dog from rewarding himself should he decide to head straight for the target without jumping.

- Have a friend entice your dog with a toy or treat from a position beyond the last obstacle.

- Have a friend restrain your dog at the start to provide added incentive and impulsion over the jumps.

- Use a toy-on-a-stick to help the dog focus ahead.

TRAINING TIP: Never be afraid to use training aids such as targets, wire guides, or toys. Once your dog has been rewarded for the behavior you desire, you can soon eliminate the extra help. Because the behavior you want has been patterned, your dog will most likely perform correctly even after the training aids have been removed. Then, you can easily couple the behavior with the command and body cues you want to use to get that behavior.

Using a toy-on-a-stick can help a dog focus ahead when first learning to sequence.

After only a few repetitions, you can usually eliminate the extra help.

NIPPING AND BARKING

Nipping and barking usually result from frustration on the part of the dog. Often the cause is that the handler's commands are given too late. Other times, the dog is faster than the handler — but the handler insists on trying to run close to the dog rather than handling from at least a moderate distance. (Nipping is especially common for herding breeds, since it is a natural herding instinct when the dog is working close to the stock. Working at more of a distance helps in cases such as these.)

If you experience nipping and/or barking, shorten up your sequence to no more than two obstacles. Reward the dog only for completing the sequence smoothly and without nipping or barking. Gradually add one obstacle at a time. Never progress, however, until the previous sequence is perfectly smooth and quiet.

As a general rule, try to stay at least several feet away from the wings and don't lean over to give your signals. If your dog is reluctant to work with you at a moderate distance, try using a toy-on-a stick. This will keep you from crowding the wings and will allow your body posture to remain upright. You may also want to review your work on calling and sending to individual obstacles, as described in *Book 1: Obstacle Training*. If you have completed this important foundation work, you will be unlikely to encounter problems with working at a distance in your sequencing.

When you and your dog become accustomed to working at a moderate distance and you start giving your commands on time as a matter of habit, you will most likely find that your dog no longer nips or barks.

How to Progress

Once you are successfully completing the exercise without leading out, start behind the dog. This will simulate the many situations you will encounter on a course in which the dog is already ahead of you as you approach a straight-line sequence of jumps.

Be sure to work the exercise off both the right and the left. Eventually progress to larger spacing between obstacles, until you can successfully perform the exercise when the jumps are spaced 25 - 30 feet apart.

Then, substitute spread jumps for one or more of the single jumps. Eventually, set the jumps at angles, while still maintaining straight-line sequences.

> **NOTE:** *When using spread jumps in your sequences, be sure to provide a minimum of 21 feet both before and after the spread jump to allow adequate room for take-off and landing.*

Call-Offs

Once you have patterned a sequence and the dog is performing well, it is time to inject a **call-off**. In a call-off, you will ask the dog to turn toward you rather than taking an obstacle that is directly in his path. Teaching call-offs is an essential step in communicating to the dog that you want him to follow your commands and body cues — not decide for himself which obstacle to take next.

To call the dog off an incorrect obstacle in his path you will use your *Come!* command (or whatever command you have trained to indicate *"come to me quickly on my first and only command")* coupled with a body cue. Your body cue will vary depending on where you are going next. It is very important that your body cue appears very different to the dog from the cue you would use to direct your dog toward the obstacle in his path. For a call-off at the end of an exercise, you will turn to face the dog and back up, as if performing a recall.

> **TRAINING TIP:** *Once your dog has learned to sequence, he will find that soaring from one obstacle to the next is great fun. To avoid any future problems with your dog being reluctant to call-off any obstacle in his path, you want to make call-offs extremely rewarding for the dog. To instill an early love of the call-off, give extra-special rewards for speedy responses. Throw a toy or food container between your legs as your dog comes barreling toward you, or engage in a special game of chase, keep-away, or tug-of-war.*

HOW TO BEGIN

Position yourself and your dog as if you were going to perform the three-jump straight-line sequence (Figure 3-4). When your dog is in mid-air over jump #2, give your *Come!* command as you turn to face your dog and back up. Reward generously for coming. If successful, practice the same sequence off your right.

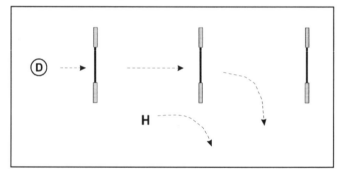

Figure 3-4: Calling the dog off the third jump.

If your dog ignores your command and continues ahead, give your verbal correction and do one of the following:

- Physically block alternative paths before the next try so that your dog will be successful.

- Calmly take your dog's tab (don't chase him or lunge at him) and remind him what "*Come!*" means. Say *Come!*

then pop and release (don't drag!) him towards you followed by lavish praise and an opportunity to try the exercise again. If your dog repeats his mistake on the next try, your *Come!* reminder was not significant enough for your dog.

Sequences with Tunnels

In the straight-line sequence shown in Figure 3-5, the dog performs the jump, the open tunnel, and then the closed tunnel.

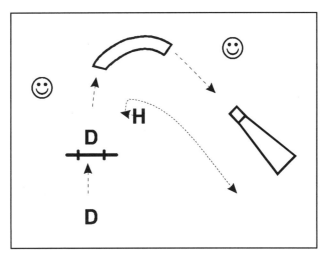

Figure 3-5: Straight-line sequence using tunnels.

Although the sequence may not appear to be a straight line from the point of view of the handler, it does appear so to the dog. When the dog is in mid-air over the first jump, he is directly in line with the tunnel opening. When he exits the open tunnel, the closed tunnel is directly in view. No turns are required, so the exercise is considered a straight-line sequence. As with the last exercise, you should master a two-obstacle sequence before progressing to three obstacles.

How to Begin

Place your dog in a sit-stay behind the open tunnel and lead out. Choose a landmark such as a tree or post that is roughly mid-way between the dog's current position and the tunnel opening. Give your *Tunnel!* command and move toward your landmark, taking only small steps so that you won't reach the tunnel opening before your dog. (If you do, you will be forced to stop moving, which may cause your dog to stop moving as well.)

If you get too close to the tunnel, you will also be tempted to start moving away before your dog is committed, because you have no place else to move. This can cause your dog to pull out with you as you start to move away.

> **NOTE:** *In our classes we often use "smiley face" markers on stands as visible landmarks to help students point their bodies in the right direction. These smiley faces, also referred to as path markers or push-point landmarks, are indicated throughout this book by the ☺ symbol.*

When sequencing with tunnels, give your next command before your dog emerges from the tunnel exit. (Photo: Tien Tran Photography)

Along with your command you should simultaneously give a clear, steady signal with your flat palm facing toward your landmark — as if pushing on the air in the direction of the landmark would help propel the dog in the direction you desire. As soon as your dog enters the tunnel, back up several steps. As he exits, give your command and signal for the closed tunnel while taking small steps toward a point between the open-tunnel exit and the closed-tunnel entrance. Praise and reward for a job well done.

If all goes well, progress to three obstacles. Leave your dog behind the first jump and lead out to a position between the jump and tunnel. Facing the path between the dog and the first jump, command and signal the jump. When the dog is in mid air over the jump, give your *Tunnel!* command as you smoothly take small steps toward a point between the jump and the tunnel opening. Do not face or point to the tunnel opening, or your dog will be uncertain of your wishes.

As soon as the dog has entered the tunnel, back up. When he exits, give your command and signal for the closed tunnel while moving toward a point between the open-tunnel exit and the closed-tunnel entrance. Praise and reward.

KEEP YOUR HANDLING SMOOTH

Throughout all of your sequencing, work hard to keep your movements smooth and fluid. Your signals should be steady and deliberate, and then released slowly and smoothly. Choppy, jerky signals can easily take your dog's attention away from his forward moving path. It may help to imagine that you are handling in a sea of molasses, where no flailing, wild, or choppy movements are possible.

> **VERY IMPORTANT NOTE:** *Although you may be able to direct your dog to perform these simple sequences by running up to each obstacle instead of using careful body cues, it is important to use the cues. The beauty of the cues you are developing (using your small steps, facing the path rather than the obstacle, etc.) is that they will work regardless of your distance from the dog. The same body movements and signals you give three feet away from your dog will eventually work when you are 30 feet from the dog. What's more, they will also work if there are one or more obstacles between you and the dog. There will be no need to retrain or to confuse your dog by changing your method of communication when you work at a distance. If you choose, instead, to communicate which obstacle to take by running up to each obstacle, the dog learns to take the obstacle that's closest to you. This strategy may work for you on simple sequences, however, you will probably experience trouble when you encounter longer and more complex sequences. The bottom line is: train the cues from the start to lay a solid foundation in communication. Once learned, they will work for you in all situations – near or far.*

If You Have Problems...

INAPPROPRIATE BODY CUES

... Your dog may have **bypassed one of the tunnels.** Although the problem may have been caused by late commands, it is most likely due to your body language. If you face the tunnel opening rather than the intended path, you may cue the dog to bypass the tunnel (Figure 3-6). Try the exercise again, making an effort to face the path rather than the obstacle.

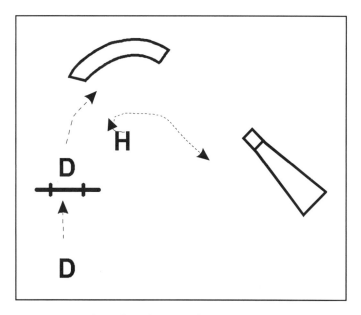

Figure 3-6: If you face the tunnel opening, rather than the path, your dog may bypass the correct opening.

Another problem can occur **if you meet your dog at the tunnel exit**. If you do, your path will be pulling away from the next obstacle, which may draw the dog away with you (Figure 3-7). It is always better to be wide moving inward rather than close moving outward. Try the sequence again, without running in close to the open-tunnel exit.

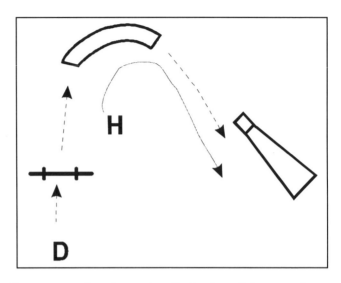

Figure 3-7: A diverging path pulls the dog off the next obstacle.

How to Progress

Once your dog has caught on, reduce your lead-out until he can perform the sequence while you remain behind the first jump (Figure 3-8).

You have now developed a skill that will allow your dog to run at his full speed while you move ahead to direct him as he exits the chute.

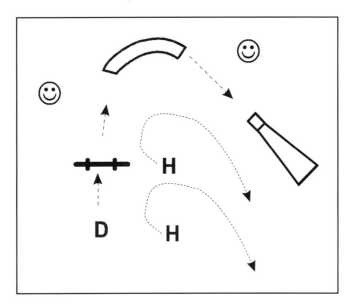

Figure 3-8: Reduce your lead-out until you are remaining behind the first jump for the entire sequence. Remember to face the path, indicated by the smiley faces, when the dog is in mid-air over the jump, and when he exits the tunnel.

CALL-OFFS

There will be many instances where you don't want your dog to take the obstacle that is directly in front of him. Since we have patterned and rewarded the dog for performing this sequence, it's the perfect time to try a call-off.

Begin with the first two obstacles as you did earlier. When the dog exits the open tunnel, command *Come!* while backing up and turning to face him.

While training, if your dog doesn't come on your first command, don't give additional commands. This only teaches the dog that coming to you is optional. Instead, calmly get the dog. You may want to remind him what *Come!* means by giving him a come correction, followed by praise. Help your dog be successful on the next try by blocking alternatives to coming with wire guides or other barriers. Then repeat only the part of the sequence where the mistake was made. Reward him well, and quit for the time being. Make a point to work on your instant recalls with distractions away from your agility training.

> **IMPORTANT NOTE:** *Always insist on a reliable recall before sequencing. To maintain your dog's happy attitude toward agility, you want to make as few corrections as possible during your training sessions. The alternative, allowing your dog to continue ahead or wander while you repeat your Come! command incessantly, is even more detrimental to your agility training — not to mention to your dog and handler working relationship.*

Sequences with the Pause Table

In another straight-line sequence, the dog starts with the tire, continues to the table, then returns through the tire (Figure 3-9).

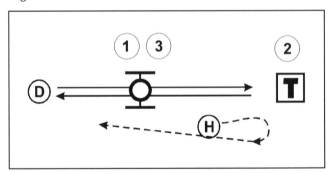

Figure 3-9: Straight-line sequence using the pause table.

Lead out and give your *Tire!* command. When your dog is in mid-air, give your *Table!* command. No later than the moment all four feet touch the table, give your command to down or sit.

During the table count, back away from the obstacle. When the judge says *Go!*, give your *Tire!* command. Move forward with your shoulders facing inward, taking a slightly converging path without running into the tire frame.

> **TRAINING TIP:** *When calling the dog off the table, don't use a release word or the dog's name in addition to the Tire! command. These extra words don't provide the dog with any useful information, and they waste time.*

If you were successful, gradually reduce your lead-out at the start. This will simulate the times on the course when you will not be able to get ahead of your dog as he approaches the table. Also, gradually increase your lead-out during the table count (Figure 3-10). The ability to lead out at the table is a valuable skill, particularly with a fast dog. Leading out can give you the advantage of showing the dog exactly where he will be going, resulting in a faster, smoother performance.

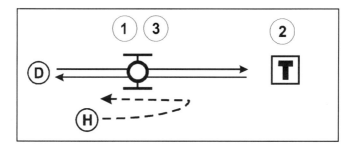

Figure 3-10: Progress by reducing your lead-out at the start and increasing your lead-out at the table.

If You Have Problems...

...Your dog may have **bypassed the tire or table** because you ran in too close and then pulled away (Figure 3-11).

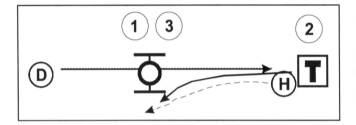

Figure 3-11: Hovering near the table causes a runout at the tire.

If you hover near the table until the count is completed, your path will be pulling away from the tire. When you hover, you are also giving no advance information to the dog about which obstacle is next. As a result, when you release him from the table he is likely to be momentarily confused about where to go, which can cause a runout and/or lost time. Try the exercise again, this time leading out from the table.

...Your dog may have **ignored your command to *Sit!* or *Down!*** If this happens, don't give additional commands, as this only convinces your dog that your command is optional.

Instead, help him get it right by placing him in the correct position, followed by praise, release, and an opportunity to try again. Then make it a point to practice the down or sit later, away from agility, on a variety of surfaces and with a variety of distractions.

> ***TRAINING TIP:*** *Avoid excessive manhandling of your dog on the pause table. You may inadvertently train him to avoid the obstacle completely. Address any problems with the sit or down away from agility on a variety of surfaces, using whatever incentives and corrections are necessary to achieve the desired results.*

…Your dog may have **downed instantly** on the table **but stayed there** when you gave your next obstacle command. This can cause many lost seconds in the agility course. If this happens, don't repeat your command or use his name or a release word. If you do, your dog will be training you to beg him to get off the table while the seconds tick by.

Instead, if your first command is ignored, help him get it right with a motivational pop toward the obstacle using his tab. Follow with abundant praise and an immediate opportunity to try again.

Sequences with Contact Obstacles

When you begin sequencing with contact obstacles, position the contact obstacle at the beginning or in the middle of the sequence, rather than at the end. This will give you an opportunity to work on fast, smooth transitions from the bottom of the contact zone to the next obstacle.

You may also find it helpful to use wire guides, hoops, food treats, or targets to help ensure the dog will perform the contact obstacles correctly.

Set up a straight-line sequence as shown in Figure 3-12.

When sequencing with contact obstacles, give your command for the
next obstacle when your dog is on the contact zone.

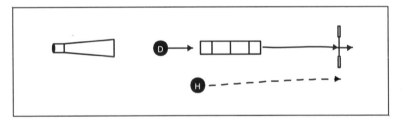

Figure 3-12: Straight-line sequence using the A-frame.

Begin by performing only the last two obstacles of the sequence. Position the dog in front of the A-frame and lead
out as shown in Figure 3-12. Start wide enough from the A-
frame that you can take a slightly converging path and not
become caught behind the wing of the last jump.

Give your command and signal for the A-frame, and begin
moving forward. When the dog reaches the down-side contact zone, command and signal the jump. Do not preface
the command with a release word or the dog's name.
These offer no useful information and delay your command

for the next obstacle. Likewise, don't preface the command with a command to *Come!* You do not want the dog to come toward you. You want him to move straight ahead to the next obstacle.

If all goes well, progress to the full three-obstacle sequence (Figure 3-13). Lead out to position H1, then gradually reduce your lead-out by starting at H2, and then H3. This will simulate the times on the course when you cannot get ahead of your dog. As you reduce your lead-out, gradually increase your parallel distance from the dog and take a slightly converging path throughout the sequence. This is particularly important with a fast dog, as he will be working ahead of you. You will then be "steering from the rear."

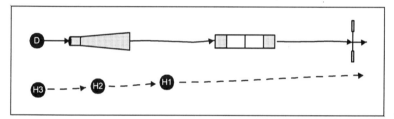

Figure 3-13: As you reduce your lead-out, gradually increase your parallel distance from your dog.

If You Have Problems...

INAPPROPRIATE BODY CUES

... Your dog may have **bypassed the A-frame.** If you start too close to your dog rather than starting from a wider handling position, your dog is likely to exit the chute ahead of you. Because you will be taking a slightly diverging path, this can cue the dog to pull out from the A-frame, especially if you are behind him as he exits (Figure 3-14). Try again, starting from a wider handling position.

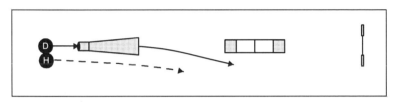

Figure 3-14: Diverging handling path causes a runout at the A-frame.

…Your dog may have **bypassed the A-frame, even though your handling path and command timing were good.** If your dog is fast and he exits the chute ahead of you, he may not yet possess the confidence to continue ahead as you steer from the rear. To help the dog be correct, before beginning the exercise, show the dog a large treat placed on the last slat (those using *Spot!*) or on a target on the ground (those using *Bottom!* or *All the Way!*). On your next attempt, your dog is likely to continue ahead smoothly. Soon, you will be able to wean him off the treat.

…Your dog may have **bypassed the jump** (Figure 3-15). In this sequence, if you run in too close to the contact zone, you will be forced to pull out to the right to avoid getting trapped behind the jump wing. This could easily cue your dog to run around it as well. Try the exercise again, taking a wider path at the contact zone.

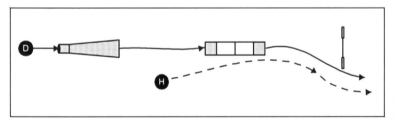

Figure 3-15: Diverging handling path causes a runout at the jump.

POOR RELEASE FROM THE CONTACT ZONE

…Your dog may have **failed to move ahead immediately from the contact to the jump.** If this occurs, don't repeat your command to jump. This will only put you in a position of begging as precious seconds tick away. You want your dog to understand that he must move ahead on your first and only command. Instead, calmly return to him, take his tab and give him a quick, motivational pop and release toward the correct obstacle or direction. Follow the correct performance with lots of praise and an immediate opportunity to try again.

> **NOTE:** *If you have placed food on the contact — even if the dog has not yet finished eating all of the food — the opportunity to eat it is a very limited-time offer. When you give a command for the next obstacle, your dog should be expected to leave the plank immediately, without hesitation. This is easy to train if you are fair and always consistent.*

Sequences with Weave Poles

For your beginning sequencing work, you may find it helpful to use training weave poles, such as the offset poles, rather than regulation poles. Since the skill you are working on is sequencing, not weave-pole training, you should do everything possible to make it likely that your dog's weave-pole performance will be fast and accurate.

When you first start sequencing with weave poles, position them at the beginning of the sequence, rather than at the middle or end. It is easier to successfully enter the weave poles from a standstill, rather than at speed. As your dog progresses, you can begin to position the poles within the sequence. Use wire guides or other barriers to make it easy for the dog to enter correctly. Eventually you can remove the guides.

Set up a sequence with weave poles as shown in Figure 3-16. First perform only the last two obstacles of the sequence. If successful, perform all three obstacles (Figure 3-

17). Start by leading out to position H1 and gradually reduce your lead-out to positions H2 and H3.

For the weave poles, give your command for the next obstacle when the dog's nose is just beginning to pass the last pole.

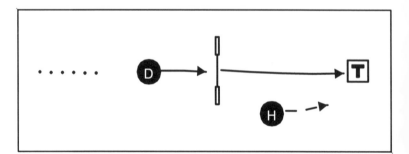

Figure 3-16: Straight-line sequence using weave poles.

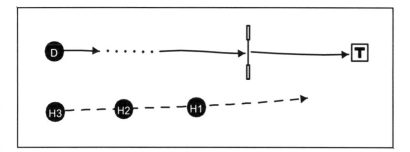

Figure 3-17: As you reduce your lead-out, gradually increase your parallel distance from your dog.

If You Have Problems...

INAPPROPRIATE BODY CUES

... Your dog may have **bypassed the jump** (Figure 3-18). If you start too close to your dog, you will pull away from the jump as you move forward. Your dog may interpret this as a cue to pull away with you. Try again, starting from a wider handler position.

...Your dog may have taken the jump but **bypassed the table** (Figure 3-19). As in the previous example, this is often caused by starting too close to your dog. This is especially likely if your dog is much faster than you are. Try again, starting from a wider handling position.

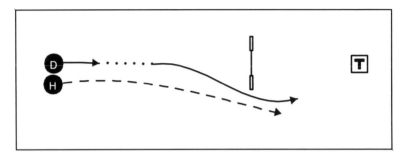

Figure 3-18: Diverging handling path causes a runout at the jump.

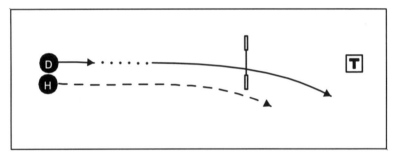

Figure 3-19: Diverging handling path causes a runout at the table.

…Your dog may have **bypassed the table, despite good handling on your part**. Your dog may not have the confidence to move ahead of you toward the table. If this happens, place a treat on a target on the back side of the table. Show it to your dog but don't let him have it. On your next attempt, your dog is likely to continue ahead smoothly. Soon, you will be able to wean him off the target.

Additional Straight–Line Sequences

Continue to put together two- and three-obstacle straight-line sequences using different combinations of obstacles. Start each new sequence by leading out to make it easier for your dog to be successful, and then gradually start farther back with your dog working ahead of you. This will simulate the times on the course when you can't get ahead of your dog. You can also work to gradually increase your parallel distance from your dog.

The following are some examples of sequences to practice. Work them off the left and off the right, forward and backwards, and then gradually increase the distance between the obstacles. Don't forget to practice call-offs at unexpected moments, as well. Reward generously for responding immediately!

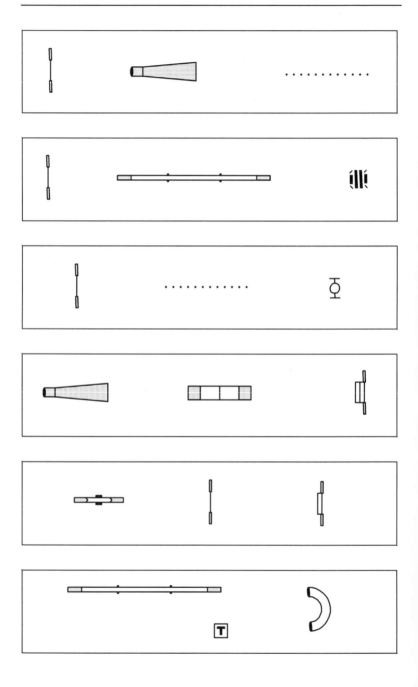

4 Turn Sequences

Having mastered three-obstacle straight-line sequences, it's time to begin training turns. You will need to turn your dog whenever the next obstacle is not within the dog's direct path and view. To turn your dog toward you, you will turn your shoulder and give your *Come!* command — a command that you have already thoroughly trained to mean "come quickly and immediately on my first and only command." The moment your dog has turned his head and can see the correct obstacle, you will give him the command for that obstacle. In this way, you are interrupting your *Come!* command with the command for the next obstacle. If you did not interrupt the *Come!* command, you would expect the dog to come all the way to you.

For turns away from the handler, you will use an *Out!* command, rather than a *Come!* command. These outward turns are described in *Chapter 6*.

> **TRAINING TIP:** *You may discover that your dog will sometimes execute a turn even without your using a Come! command. This is particularly true when you are close to your dog. Even if you think your dog might turn without your saying Come! it is best to command <u>every</u> turn. You will get more immediate, tighter turns (which translate to faster times). You will also greatly reduce the likelihood that your dog will misunderstand your intentions and continue ahead to an incorrect obstacle.*

Begin with the arrangement of jumps shown in Figure 4-1. The unnumbered fourth jump is positioned to present an alternative to the dog.

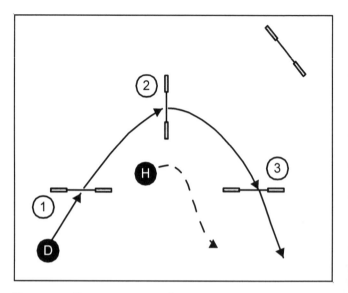

Figure 4-1: Turn sequence with jumps.

Set your dog up so that he is in line with the first two jumps. Lead out past the first jump, being careful to remain outside the wing. Command and signal your dog to take the first two jumps. When your dog is mid-air over jump #2, turn to your right (standing upright and "steering" with your shoulders) and command *Come!*. When his head turns to see the jump #3, give your jump command and signal.

> **TRAINING TIP:** Give your command as soon as your dog sees the correct obstacle. Don't wait until the dog looks at you — it's "crunchy" and it wastes time. Moreover, by the time he looks back at the correct obstacle after looking at you, it may be too late to perform the obstacle without incurring a penalty for a knocked bar or a runout.

If You Have Problems

...Your dog may have **bypassed the last jump**. This could happen if your *Come!* command was late. This is a common mistake for novice handlers.

When handling turns, your timing is critical. You must give your *Come!* command while the dog is completing the previous obstacle. For jumps, this means when the dog is in mid-air. If you wait until after the dog lands, (or completely exits the tunnel, or leaves the contact obstacle, etc.) your *Come!* command will likely cause the dog to take an overly wide path or bypass the correct obstacle.

Another reason your dog may have bypassed the last jump is that your handling path may have taken you into the wing of the last jump (Figure 4-2). This forces you to pull away from the jump at the last moment, which can often cue your dog to do the same.

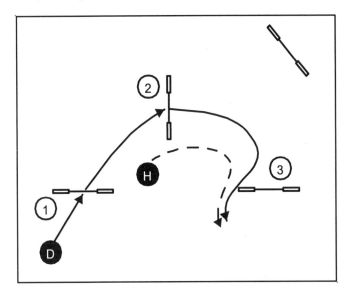

Figure 4-2: Diverging handling path causes a runout at jump #3.

If your dog bypasses the last jump despite good handling on your part, the problem may be due to a lack of confidence on the part of your dog. On your next attempt, try throwing a toy or food container with your signaling hand as you give your command for the last jump, or use the toy-on-a-stick. Remember to release to the toy with a command to *Get it!*

...Your dog may have **failed to turn,** continuing ahead to the incorrect jump (Figure 4-3). If you are moving forward without turning your shoulder as you say *Come!*, most dogs will continue straight ahead. Body language usually wins out over verbal commands when the two conflict. Try the exercise again, making an effort to cease forward movement and to turn your shoulder as you say *Come!*

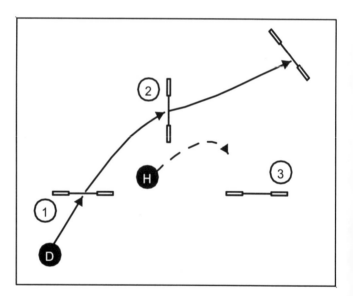

Figure 4-3: The dog continues ahead when the handler fails to hang back and turn.

Another reason your dog might fail to turn, taking the incorrect jump in his path, is if your *Come!* command was late. If this was the case, try again, this time giving your *Come!*

command and turning your shoulder when your dog is in mid-air over jump #2.

How to Progress

As soon as your dog is sequencing smoothly, begin working at more of a distance. This will allow your dog to move ahead at his fastest speed and will greatly increase your handling options.

Gradually reduce your lead-out and remain farther back each time until you are staying behind a line made by the first jump (Figure 4-4).

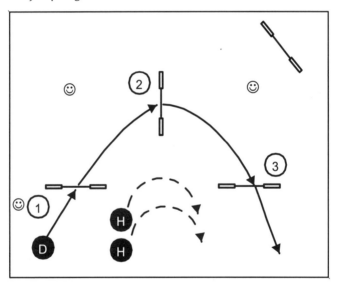

Figure 4-4: Gradually decrease your lead-out and increase your parallel distance from the dog.

As you gain distance, it will be increasingly important to face the paths (indicated by ☺) rather than the obstacles themselves as you give your commands. This will help eliminate any ambiguity about where you want your dog to go.

For example, when you give your command for jump #1, you should face between the dog and jump #1. When your dog is in mid-air over jump #1, you should face between jump #1 and jump #2. Likewise, when you give your command for jump #3 you should be facing between jump #2 and jump #3.

The signal you give along with your command will be a flat palm gently pressing toward the path marker, since this will be the most visible signal from your dog's perspective.

As you give your commands and signals, keep your feet moving in small, fluid steps. If you suddenly stop moving, your dog may also stop moving or may hesitate.

Call-Offs

Once you have mastered the turn sequence, try a call-off. Begin with the first two jumps as before. However, when your dog is in mid-air above jump #2, command *Come!* while backing up and turning to face the dog (Figure 4-5). Remember to stand up straight and turn your shoulder away from the path to the third jump. Don't bend forward at the waist. This only serves to push the dog away from you.

> **TRAINING TIP:** *Whenever your dog is faced with a tempting incorrect obstacle, ask yourself what body cue you would use if you wanted your dog to take the incorrect obstacle? Then make sure the cue you are giving for the correct choice looks very different to the dog.*

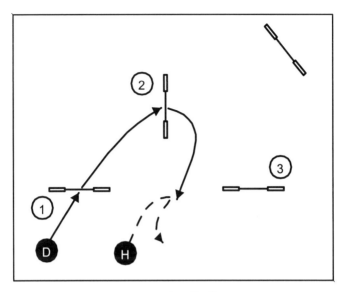

Figure 4-5: Turn sequence with call-off.

If You Have Problems

...Your dog may have **continued over jump #3**, rather than coming to you. This may happen if your command is late. If this is the case, work with a friend to help improve the timing of your commands.

This may also happen if you step forward or bend forward at the waist rather than stepping backward and remaining upright as you call. When your verbal command and body cues conflict, your dog will be likely to follow your body cues. On your next attempt, make an effort to turn your shoulder and remain upright as you say *Come!*

Your dog may have continued over jump #3, even though your command timing and body cues were perfect. Your dog has simply failed to respond to your cues. On the next attempt, block alternatives to coming by having someone stand in front of jump #3, or by using a barrier. Give a jackpot reward for getting it right on the next try.

As an alternative to using a barrier, you could give a come reminder (calmly take the dog's tab, say *Come!,* pop and release toward you as you back up, followed by lots of sincere praise). Give your dog an immediate opportunity to try again. If he is successful, give an extra special reward. If the dog is still unsuccessful— despite perfect handling on your part — your *Come!* reminder was not significant enough to make a change in behavior.

Practice Variations on a Theme

After a successful call-off, it's often a good idea to immediately repeat the original sequence without the call-off, to emphasize the difference in cues you will give for each variation. Practicing variations on a theme is a wonderful way to encourage your dog to pay attention, and to keep him from operating on autopilot. In the sequence you just completed, you may want to direct the dog over the straight line of jumps (jumps #1, #2, and the unnumbered jump) and then try the turn to jump #3 on your next try. When you can get the variation you want each time on your first attempt, you will know you are communicating clearly and developing all-important teamwork with your dog.

Once you have mastered this turn sequence with call-offs and variations, practice the same sequence in a mirror-image off your right.

How to Progress

Progress to working on three-obstacle turn sequences using different combinations of obstacles. To make turns after obstacles other than jumps, give your *Come!* command as the dog is completing the previous obstacle.

- After a tunnel, give your command before the dog begins to exit.

- With contacts, give your command when he has reached the contact zone.

- With weave poles, give your command the moment your dog's nose begins to pass the last pole.

Remember to practice your turn sequences as much off the right as you do off the left. Some sample turn sequences are provided below.

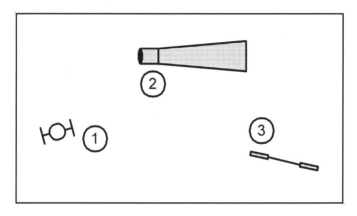

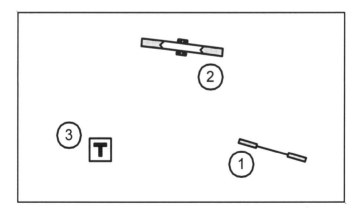

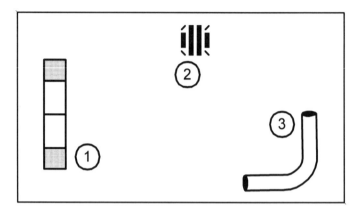

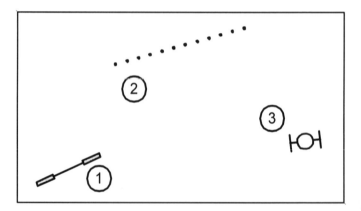

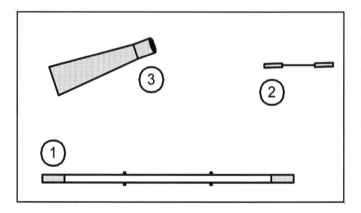

Adding Distance

On your turn exercises, remember to keep adding distance to take advantage of your dog's speed and to increase his confidence at a distance. Two sequence examples are shown in Figures 4-6 and 4-7. Begin by leading out to position H1 and work as closely as necessary to achieve a smooth sequence. Gradually decrease your lead-out to position H2 and increase the amount of parallel distance that you keep between you and your dog.

Remember to face the path markers as you give your commands. Your feet will continue moving, however, in small, controlled steps.

Because these sequences include contact obstacles and weave poles, you will now need the early distance work on these obstacles that you mastered in *Book 1: Obstacle Training*. To help your dog perform these obstacles accurately at a distance, you may want to use wire guides, hoops, or targets.

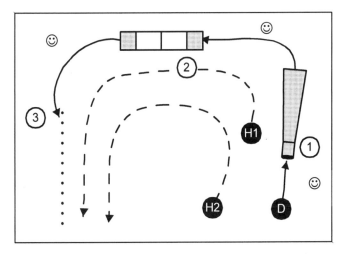

Figure 4-6: Adding distance on a turn sequence.

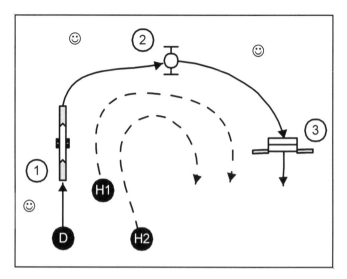

Figure 4-7: Adding distance on a turn sequence.

Sometimes, being able to handle a turn sequence at a distance can be a great advantage. In Figure 4-8, the handler's ability to handle wide allows him to be in an advantageous position to indicate the weave pole entry. As a result, the sequence is completed smoothly.

If the handler could not work at a distance for obstacles #1 – #3, he may find himself in a poor position to indicate obstacle #4 (Figure 4-9).

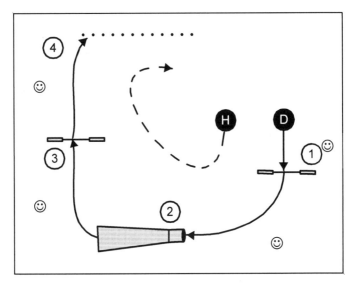

Figure 4-8: Handling wide on obstacles #1 – #3 allows the handler an advantageous position for obstacle #4.

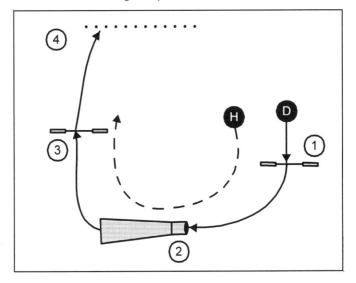

Figure 4-9: Handling close on obstacles #1 – 3 puts the handler behind and in a poor position to indicate obstacle #4.

Continuing Your Contact-Zone Training

Now that you are doing turn sequences with contact obstacles, you are ready to take your contact-zone training a step further. When you completed your contact training in *Book 1*, you were giving your *Spot!* command as your dog began his descent. He was then running quickly to the end of the obstacle and waiting for further instructions. To reward correct performance, you were alternating between having a treat already placed on the underside of the slat, going up to the dog and delivering a treat, or giving only praise.

You will now want to teach your dog that running quickly to the spot will earn him the opportunity to complete one or more obstacles for the possibility of a jackpot. By transferring the timing of your reward to an obstacle that comes after the contact obstacle, you avoid the problem of the dog realizing that there will be no food on the contacts at an actual trial. By the time he would normally expect his reward, he is already in the midst of a fast-paced sequence.

Set up a contact obstacle followed by a choice of two obstacles (Figure 4-10).

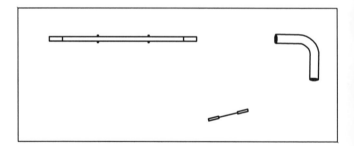

Figure 4-10: Setup for working a jackpot after a contact obstacle.

Begin the dog walk off your left and give your *Spot!* command. Your dog should run quickly down to the last slat and look at you with anticipation. Wait a moment, then, with an air of suspense, give an enthusiastic command for one of the obstacles. If you have chosen the tunnel, your command will simply be *Tunnel!* If you have chosen the jump, command *Come!* to turn the dog toward the jump, then follow with your *Jump!* command. When the dog complies, give an extra-special reward and lots of praise.

On successive tries, randomly alternate between obstacles. Your dog should now be running to the spot and looking to you for a command to the next obstacle, followed by a wonderful reward.

A week or so later, when he has caught on to the concept, add additional obstacles and delay the reward until after he completes two obstacles. From then on, randomly reward after one, two, or three, obstacles — and sometimes give only praise.

Be sure to follow the same procedure with the other contact obstacles as well.

TRAINING TIP: *In all of your sequencing with contact obstacles, don't forget that if your dog ever fails to leave a contact obstacle on your first and only command, calmly return to him, take his tab and give him a quick pop and release toward the correct obstacle or direction. Follow the correct performance with lots of sincere praise and an immediate opportunity to try again.*

Don't even THINK about entering a trial until you have mastered the side-switches.
(Top photo: Gene Abrahamson. Bottom photo: Tien Tran Photography)

<u>5</u> Side-Switches

Most agility courses cannot be handled entirely off your left or your right side. If you were to try, your dog's speed on the course would be limited to how fast you could run. Since most dogs can run faster than their owners, your dog would either slow down to match your pace or check back and spin while waiting for you to catch up with him. What's more, you would probably need a tank of oxygen each time you crossed the finish line! Thus, one of the most important sequencing skills you will need to develop are **side-switches** — critical maneuvers that allow you to switch smoothly from handling off the right to handling off the left, and vice-versa. Side-switches are essential building blocks for your foundation in sequence training.

If your goal is to develop a smooth working relationship with your dog, **don't even THINK about** running an entire course or entering a trial without having first mastered all of the side-switches! If you do, your dog is likely to develop unwanted behaviors that will result in course faults and many seconds added to your course time.

Side-Switches at Jumps

To switch sides during jump sequences, you will need to master three types of side-switches: the *cross-in-front*, the *cross-behind*, and *pull-back*. Using the set-up shown in Figure 5-1, you can train all three.

For each of the exercises, assume the course follows an "S" pattern, so you will begin by handling jump #1 off your left. Also assume the course continues to the left after jump #3, requiring you to handle jump #3 off your right.

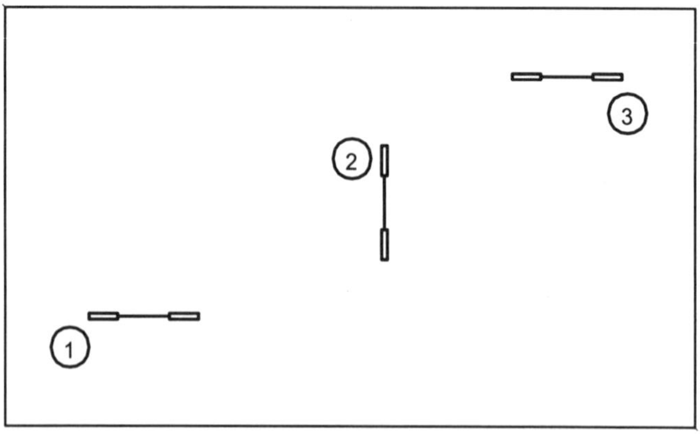

Figure 5-1: Setup for side-switching at jump.

For all of the side-switches you will start by placing your dog in a sit-stay square with the first jump rather than on an angle. (If the sequence were the start of a course, it would be beneficial to position your dog at an angle toward jump #2. For this exercise, however, we will pretend that the sequence occurs in the middle of a longer sequence that requires the dog to approach obstacle #1 squarely.)

Pull-Back

The **pull-back** side-switch (Figure 5-2) is sometimes called a **fake-out** because the handler turns in the opposite direction of the course flow for a moment, then quickly turns back on track. The only benefit of this side-switch is that it requires few skills and can be learned by most handlers in minutes. The drawback is that it is a less-than elegant maneuver that wastes time on the course. It's best to use the pull-back only when absolutely necessary, such as when you need an "emergency tool" to handle an unexpected situation.

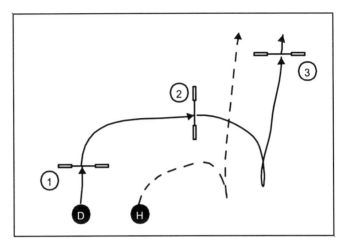

Figure 5-2: Pull-back side-switch at jump.

To try a pull-back, position your dog squarely with the first jump and direct him through a right turn from jumps #1 to #2. When the dog is in mid-air over #2, give a *Come!* command and rotate your body clockwise as if you were making another 90-degree right turn.

When the dog reaches your left side, pivot 180 degrees counterclockwise, towards your dog. This will cause your dog to turn 180 degrees as well, so you will both be facing jump #3, and your dog will be on your right. As soon as he is facing #3, give your command to jump and move forward, taking a slightly converging path toward the left edge of the wing of jump #3.

IF YOU HAVE PROBLEMS...

...Your dog may have **failed to pivot tightly between jumps** #2 and #3. On your next attempt, hold a treat in your left hand and transfer it to your right hand while pulling your dog back. Give him the treat when he has reached the farthest point of the pull-back. You soon be able to eliminate the treat once your dog has caught on to the maneuver.

…Your dog may have **bypassed jump #3.** If you travel too far past #2 before pivoting, your path toward #3 will take you into the wing, forcing you to pull away from the jump. This may cause your dog to pull away as well. Plan your path for the pull-back carefully, making a tight pivot just past jump #2, and then taking a slightly converging path toward jump #3.

Now that you've learned the pull-back side-switch, put it out of your mind as quickly as possible. You will fare much better in competition if you master more efficient types of side-switches.

Cross-In-Front

A **cross-in-front**, sometimes referred as a **front cross, pirouette**, or **pivot**, is one of the most efficient and elegant side-switches. From a position ahead of the dog you can communicate the upcoming course path very clearly and with little ambiguity.

Crossing in front is only possible, however, when you can get sufficiently ahead of your dog to cross without interfering with him. If you have a small or short-strided dog, or if you can easily out-run your dog, you will typically encounter many opportunities on a course to cross in front of him. If you have a large, fast, or long-strided dog you can also take frequent advantage of crossing in front — if you can handle your dog at at least a moderate distance.

Figure 5-3 shows an example of a cross-in-front during a jump sequence. With the dog working off his left, the handler remains wide from the first three jumps to enable him to get well ahead of the dog before he takes the third jump. As the dog jumps, the handler pivots toward the dog, smoothly transfers the signal to his right hand, and handles the next two jumps off his right.

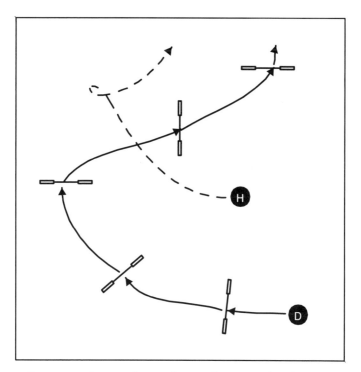

Figure 5-3: Cross-in-front side-switch executed within a course.

To train the cross-in-front, we will isolate the three-jump sequence in which the side-switch takes place, using the setup used to train the pull-back (Figure 5-4). The arrangement of the jumps used in this exercise corresponds to the last three jumps of the cross-in-front example shown in Figure 5-3.

To begin, assume you have been able to get ahead of your dog on a previous sequence (such as shown in Figure 5-3). Position yourself to handle jump #1 off the left as shown in Figure 5-4. Stand with your back to jump #2 and look over your left shoulder at your dog. Using your left hand, extend a flat hand signal that is parallel to jump #1.

Give your command to jump when the dog is mid-air, pivot to face him while stepping back and smoothly transfer your signal to your right hand. When in mid-air over jump #2, command and signal jump #3 off the right and move forward.

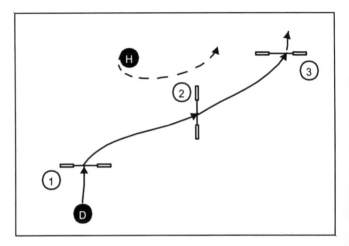

Figure 5-4: Cross-in-front side-switch between jumps. Start with your back to jump #2 and your left hand in a flat-hand signal.

IF YOU HAVE PROBLEMS...

...Your dog may have **bypassed jump #2**.This can happen if you face jump #2 rather than the path (between jumps 1 and 2) when your dog is in mid-air over jump #1. Try again, making a point to face the path rather than the jump.

A few dogs may bypass #2 even though you have handled the sequence well. If this is the case, you will need to work on your dog understanding your cue for jump #2. Work on the sequence of jump #1 to jump #2 only. Find a toy or use a food container that you can throw. Set your dog and yourself up as before, by leading out and handling the first jump off your left. Place the toy in your signaling (left) hand. Command the dog to *Jump!*, quickly transfer the toy to your right hand and throw it over jump #2 as you give the command for jump #2. Follow with a release command to *Get it!*. Repeat several times until your dog understands the maneuver. You soon will be able to eliminate the toy.

...Your dog may have **bypassed jump #3.**This can happen if you don't lead out far enough past jump #1 (Figure 5-5). The farther ahead you are to start, the smoother and faster your side-switch will be. Try the exercise again, leading out a greater distance.

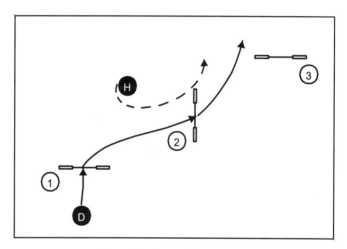

Figure 5-5: Insufficient lead-out affects handling path, leading to runout.

BLIND CROSS

A type of front cross, the **blind cross,** is different in that instead of facing the dog during the side-switch, the handler presents his back to the dog and switches signaling hands. The dog then meets up with the handler on the opposite side. Like the cross-in-front, this side-switch is only possible when you can get ahead of your dog.

A disadvantage to the blind cross is that it requires you to momentarily take your eyes off your dog. If your dog does not follow the path you intended or is faster than you expected, it can be very difficult to recover, since you have lost contact with him visually for at least a brief moment. If you do blind crosses in front of weave poles and contact obstacles, you may not know whether your dog has completed the obstacle correctly.

A blind cross, however, can be useful to someone who routinely runs close to and slightly ahead of their dog throughout the course. The handler can keep running at full speed without having to slow down to pivot and face their dog.

Cross–Behind

Like the cross-in-front, the **cross-behind**, also referred to as the **rear cross**, is an extremely useful, fast, and efficient type of side-switch. If your dog moves at even a moderate rate of speed, you will need to have this maneuver in your handling arsenal.

To do it well, the cross-behind requires precision handling as well as skill and confidence on the part of the dog. Executed poorly, the cross-behind can result in refusals, knocked bars, spins, and turns in the wrong direction. Because of its potential value, perfecting the cross-behind should be a very high-priority goal in your sequence-training program.

Your path and body language are critical when crossing behind your dog. Jerky motions, stopping abruptly, and running too close to the obstacle you are crossing behind can all foil your best efforts at completing a smooth side-switch.

You don't want to be ahead of the dog when crossing behind, so start parallel with him rather than leading out (Figure 5-6). Command and signal the first jump with your left hand and move inward toward the jump wing. When your dog is in mid-air over jump #1, give a *Come!* command and turn your body tightly to the right with a pivot in place. When your dog's head has turned to see jump #2, give your *Jump!* command and signal with your left hand, taking very small, controlled steps as the dog moves ahead of you. As the dog commits to the jump, smoothly cross behind him and transfer your signal to your opposite hand. Command the last jump and continue forward at a normal pace.

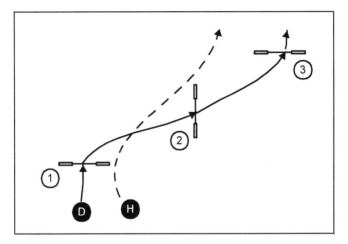

Figure 5-6: Cross-behind side-switch at jump.

TRAINING TIP: *When crossing behind your dog with any obstacle, be sure to give your obstacle command in a timely manner and use a confident, enthusiastic tone of voice. If you sound tentative and uncertain, your dog will tend to be also.*

IF YOU HAVE PROBLEMS...

... You may have gotten a **spin after jump #2**. This may have been caused by handling too close to jump #2 (Figure 5-7). Your dog must make his decision about which way to turn no later than when he is directly above the jump bar. To ensure a smooth turn to the left, you need to be positioned to the left of center of jump #2 by the time he makes his decision. This is not possible if you run up too close to the jump. Handling too close to the jump may also result in your dog bypassing jump #3, as shown in Figure 5-

7. Try the sequence again, this time crossing farther back from the jump.

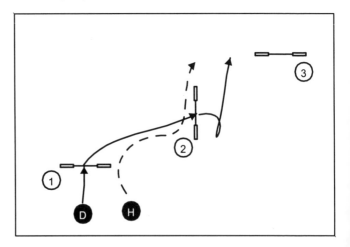

Figure 5-7: Handling too close to jump #2 causes a spin and a runout.

…Your dog may have **bypassed jump #2** by running to the left of it. This may have been caused by your switched signaling hands before your dog was ahead of you. This can result in your turning away from the path you want your dog to take, which may cause him to turn away as well. It also increases the likelihood that you will encroach upon your dog's path. Try the exercise again, maintaining a continuous signal for jumps #1 and #2. This helps keep you out of the dog's path and provides smooth continuity, as if politely telling your dog, "after you!" It also conforms to two of the consistent cues you've developed to communicate with your dog: always signaling with the hand closest to the dog, and always facing the path you want him to take. Because it conforms to your consistent set of cues, your dog is likely to understand immediately what you want him to do.

…Your **dog may lack the confidence** to jump ahead of you. If this happens, lower the jump and entice him from the opposite side of the jump with a toy or a target. Then, gradually fade away the extra help.

DROP-BEHIND

The **drop-behind** side-switch is a variation of the cross-behind side-switch. The drop-behind differs in that you are crossing behind the dog after he has completed an obstacle (such as on the landing side of a jump) rather than as he is completing the obstacle. This side-switch is most applicable for moderately paced dogs who run close to their handlers, although occasionally it can be useful with faster dogs.

In a drop-behind, you will cross behind your dog while both you and he are between the same two obstacles. (Figure 5-8). To make the side-switch, slow down to allow the dog get ahead as he jumps #2. Then, cut behind him as he lands after the jump, while commanding *Come!,* turning your shoulder, and transferring your signal to your right hand.

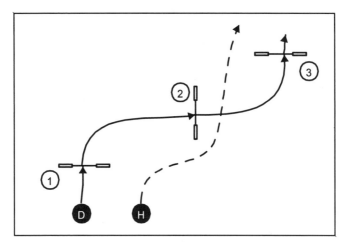

Figure 5-8: Drop-behind side-switch between two jumps.

Side-Switches at Tunnels

When switching sides at tunnels you can choose to cross in front or behind. You can also cross at the tunnel entrance or at the tunnel exit.

Cross-In-Front at Tunnel Entrance

Whenever you can get far enough ahead of your dog, crossing in front is an elegant solution (Figure 5-9). From a position ahead of the dog, you can most easily communicate the path you want your dog to take. To be able to cross in front, you will need to be able to accurately assess your speed in relation to your dog's speed. That is, you will need to know that you can get ahead of the dog and cross in front without cutting it too closely. If you don't make it to your intended position in time, you may be faulted for a dog-handler collision, or you may push the dog to an incorrect obstacle.

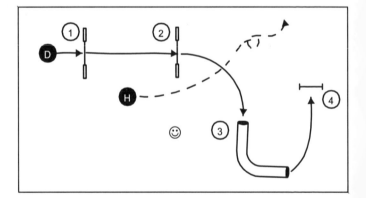

Figure 5-9: Cross-in-front side-switch at tunnel entrance.

When crossing in front, always face your dog so that you can see him the moment he exits the tunnel. If you turn your back to him while crossing in front you will lose sight of him momentarily. By the time you see him again he could easily be continuing ahead on a course of his own choosing!

Get a head start on your dog on a point along the handling path. The faster your dog is in relation to you, the farther ahead you will need to lead out. Assume that you are in the middle of a sequence and have been able to get ahead of your dog. As such, you will be handling jumps #1 and #2 off your left.

When your dog is in mid-air over jump #2, rotate counter-clockwise, facing the dog and smoothly transfer your signal to your right hand. Give your *Tunnel!* command as you take very small, controlled steps facing a point halfway between jump #2 and the tunnel opening. For the smoothest side-switch, try to stay at least five feet away from the tunnel.

Once your dog has entered the tunnel, don't feel compelled to run to the exit to meet him. While your dog is in the tunnel you have the perfect opportunity to get ahead of your dog to clearly show him the upcoming obstacle path. When your dog exits the tunnel give a *Come!* command to turn him toward the next obstacle, followed by an immediate command to jump when your dog 's head has turned to see #4.

IF YOU HAVE PROBLEMS...

...Your dog may have **gotten ahead of you,** preventing you from crossing in front. On your next try you will need to lead out a greater distance. This should indicate to you that if this sequence were in the middle of a course you would need to handle the previous sequence at more of a distance to be able to cross in front at the tunnel.

...Your dog may have **bypassed the tunnel opening** (Figure 5-10). This can happen if you face the tunnel opening rather than the path you want the dog to take (e.g., the point between jump #2 and the tunnel opening).

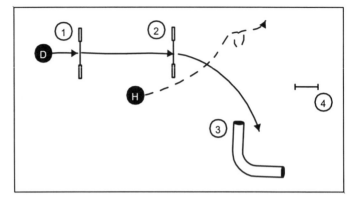

Figure 5-10: Facing the tunnel opening rather than the path can lead to a runout.

Cross-Behind

There will be times on a course when you need to switch sides but you can't get ahead of your dog as he approaches the tunnel. In these cases, your best bet is to cross behind. As it is when crossing behind jumps, your body position and handling path are very important when crossing behind a tunnel.

Using the setup shown in Figure 5-11, start parallel with your dog but wide enough so that you can take a slightly converging path toward the wing of jump #2. When your dog is in mid-air over jump #2, give a *Come!* command and turn your body tightly to the right with a pivot in place. When your dog's head has turned to see the tunnel, give your *Tunnel!* command and signal with your left hand, taking very small, controlled steps as the dog moves ahead of you.

Try to stay at least five feet from tunnel opening. As the dog commits to the tunnel, smoothly cross behind him and transfer your signal to your opposite hand. Move ahead on the course to show your dog the upcoming path.

When he exits the tunnel, he will not be looking at #4. You must therefore give a *Come!* command to turn him toward the next obstacle, followed by an immediate command to *Jump!* when his head has turned to see #4.

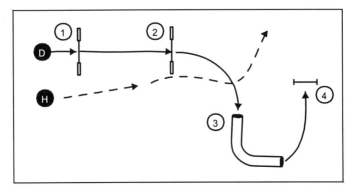

Figure 5-11: Cross-behind side-switch at tunnel entrance.

IF YOU HAVE PROBLEMS...

…Your dog may have **stopped or turned back toward you** as you attempted to cross behind. This may have been caused by your running up too close to the tunnel opening and stopping. In a similar fashion, running flat-footed is noisy and may distract or frighten your dog. When crossing behind any obstacle, stay as far behind as possible and try to run silently on the balls of your feet. Take small, controlled steps so that you will not reach the tunnel opening ahead of your dog and be forced to stop abruptly. Try to keep moving at all times. This requires you to plan and execute a careful handling path at a controlled pace.

If your dog was reluctant to go ahead of you to the tunnel despite your good handling, review the procedure for sending your dog to tunnels at a variety of angles and distances. This is covered in *Book 1: Obstacle Training*.

…You may have **gotten a very wide or a non-existent turn** between jump #2 and the tunnel. This can happen if you continue to move forward as you command *Come!* when the dog is in mid-air above jump #2. When your body cues and verbal cues conflict, most dogs will follow your body cues. Try the sequence again, this time hanging back and turning to your right and you give the *Come!* command.

Cross-In-Front at Tunnel Exit

Because your dog can't see you when he is in a tunnel, it's one of the easiest and most useful places to switch sides (Figure 5-12). If you can get ahead of your dog, crossing in front of a tunnel exit is often advantageous. As is true whenever you cross in front, you will need to be able to accurately assess your speed in relation to your dog's speed. That is, you will need to know that you can get ahead of the dog and cross in front without cutting it too closely. If you don't make it to your intended position in time, you may get faulted for a dog-handler collision, or you may push the dog to an incorrect obstacle.

IF YOU HAVE PROBLEMS...

...Your dog may have **bypassed the correct tunnel opening** as you attempted to run to the right side of the tunnel exit. This may have been caused by your pulling away before your dog had committed to the tunnel. It is especially likely to happen if you turn shoulders to the right sharply or abruptly as you head for the end of the tunnel. Try again, keeping your movements smoother and facing the path between jump and tunnel until your dog has committed to the correct entrance.

...Your dog may have **collided with you** as you attempted to cross in front. On your next attempt, try running faster or handling at a greater distance, so that you will be completely clear of the dog's path as he exits the tunnel.

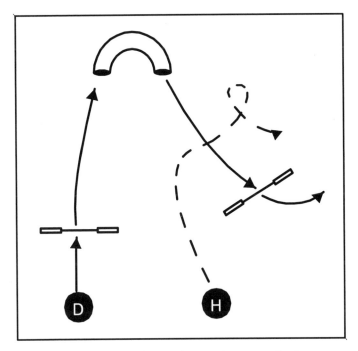

Figure 5-12: Cross-in-front side-switch at tunnel exit.

Side-Switches at Contact Obstacles

When side-switching at contact obstacles, you will generally choose to either cross in front or cross behind. You can also cross at the entrance or the exit.

Cross-In-Front at Contact Exit

When you can get a sufficient distance ahead of your dog, a cross-in-front is a good solution (Figure 5-13). Crossing in front gives you an added benefit of momentarily placing you between your dog and a possible enticing obstacle in his path. This can help deter a driven dog from choosing the next obstacle and leaving the contact prematurely.

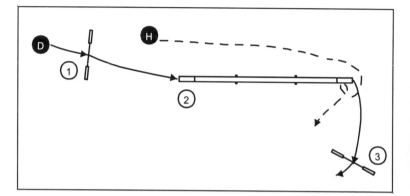

Figure 5-13: Cross-in-front side-switch at exit to contact obstacle.

If you have trained your dog to run to the end of the contact and wait until released, you will always be able to get ahead of your dog — regardless of your speed or his. Beware of wasting seconds, however, while he waits for you to cross in front of him. Placements are often separated by only tenths or even hundredths of a second. If your goal is to choose a competitive handling strategy and achieve your dog's fastest possible time, you must consider whether crossing in front will add extra seconds to your run.

Start with your dog on your right and lead out between #1 and #2. To practice this side-switch we will pretend you are in the middle of a sequence in which you are handling your dog off the right, and you are able to get somewhat ahead of him. Give your *Jump!* command and signal. When the dog is in mid-air, give your command and signal for the dog walk.

Run to the end of dog walk and cross in front, pivoting towards your dog and squaring your shoulders with him as you do. At the same time, smoothly transfer your signal from your right to your left hand.

For the fastest possible time and the least chance that your movements will interfere with the dog, try to complete your side-switch before your dog is halfway down the exit plank.

When he has reached the contact zone and you have moved into position where your dog is now on your left, give your *Come!* command and turn to your right. Give your command for the jump when his head has turned to see #3.

If you are successful, gradually reduce your lead-out until you are starting even with your dog. If your dog is faster than you are, he will reach the contact zone ahead of you and must wait until you cross in front of him.

IF YOU HAVE PROBLEMS...

...Your dog may have **bailed off the plank as you crossed in front of him.** This can happen if you fail to square your shoulders and face the dog as you are crossing in front. Cutting across the front of the plank without squaring up gives a conflicting body cue which can cause your dog to think you want him to exit the plank. Try again, this time squaring your shoulders to the dog as you cross in front.

...Your dog may have **lost time waiting for you to cross in front.** To prevent this from happening, you will need to either run faster or get a larger head start on your dog. You can often accomplish the latter by handling the approach to the dog walk at a greater distance, so that you can get further ahead. When this is not possible, your best bet may be to cross behind.

Cross-Behind at Contact Entrance

When you can't get ahead without taking extra time, a cross-behind is often a good solution (Figure 5–14). As with all cross-behinds, try to cross as far back as possible. Stopping abruptly or crossing too close to the plank can cause your dog to stop or pull off, incurring a fault.

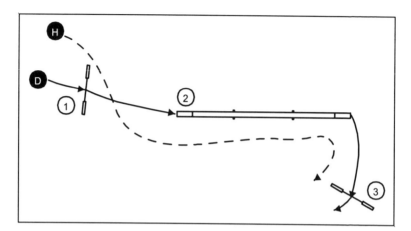

Figure 5-14: Cross-behind side-switch at entrance to contact obstacle.

Begin as if you were completing a previous sequence off the right. Start with your dog rather than leading out and position yourself wide enough from him that you will not be taking a path into the wing of the jump.

Give your command and signal for jump #1. When your dog is in mid-air, give your command for the dog walk with your right hand (the hand closest to the dog). As you move forward, use small, controlled steps to allow your dog to get ahead of you. Start to cross behind him, keeping your shoulders firmly square with the dog walk as he commits to the obstacle.

When he has committed to the dog walk, resume your normal long stride length and fast pace. Give your *Spot!* command as he begins his descent. When he has reached the contact zone, give your *Come!* command and turn to your right. Follow with your command for the jump when his head has turned to see #3.

IF YOU HAVE PROBLEMS...

...Your dog may have been **reluctant to go ahead of you** to the dog walk. If you have done your foundation work with obstacle training, your dog should already be comfortable with you sending him to any obstacle from a distance of at least 15 feet. You may want to step back in your training and work more on sending your dog to the dog walk.

To help encourage him to go ahead of you in this cross-behind exercise, show him a treat placed on the last slat (or on a target on the ground) and try the cross-behind again. If this is not a strong enough incentive, you can place the treat near the top of the upside plank, so that it will be a more visible incentive and a more immediate reward.

…Your dog may have **decided at the last minute to bypass the dog walk** rather than taking it. This can happen if you fail to keep your shoulders square with the dog walk while crossing behind. Without a conscious effort on your part to keep square, your shoulders will naturally turn to the right as you cross behind. This can cause your dog to change his mind about performing the dog walk and bail off or move to the right of it along with you. Loose or abrupt body movements can also cause your shoulder to turn, which might inadvertently change your dog's direction.

HOW TO PROGRESS

Once you have mastered side-switches at the dog walk, practice the same exercise substituting the A-frame and see-saw.

Side-Switches at Weave Poles

Because of the complex nature of weaving, side-switching on weave poles takes some time for both dog and handler to master. Before you attempt to switch sides on weave poles, your dog should be performing them off both the right and the left with accuracy, speed, and independence. You should also be able to call your dog through the weave poles and send him to the weave pole entry.

Cross-In-Front at Weave-Pole Exit

When you can get a sufficient distance ahead of your dog, a cross-in-front is a good solution (Figure 5-15). To do this, you need to be able to get ahead of the dog by at least three poles while he is weaving — without pulling him out. If you are any closer than this to your dog when you cross you are likely to draw his attention or interfere with his movement. This results in "crunchy" agility and increases the risk of a missed pole or handler contact.

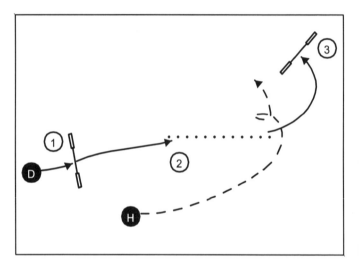

Figure 5-15: Cross-in-front side-switch at weave-pole exit.

To practice this side-switch, pretend you are in the middle of a sequence in which you are handling your dog off the left and you are able to get somewhat ahead of your dog. Start with your dog on your left, and lead out between the jump and the start of the weave poles. Give your *Jump!* command and signal. When the dog is in mid-air give your command and signal for the weave poles.

Run to the end of the weave poles and cross in front, facing your dog and squaring your shoulders with him as you do.

At the same time, smoothly transfer your signal from your left to your right hand.

As your dog's nose crosses the second-to-last pole, command *Come!* and turn left. Give your *Jump!* command when the dog's head has turned to see #3.

IF YOU HAVE PROBLEMS...

...Your dog may **have pulled out of the poles as you tried to run ahead**. Forget about crossing in front for the moment and work on being able to run ahead of the dog without pulling him out. Start slowly and progress to being able to run ahead at maximum speed. You can use wire guides to help keep the dog from making mistakes.

...Your dog may **have pulled out of the poles as you crossed in front.** Make sure you complete your cross by the time your dog is performing the third pole from the exit. If you can't make it across in time you will need to get a longer lead-out on your dog.

You may also have failed to square your shoulders as you crossed in front. Failing to do this can increase your chances that your dog will pull out prematurely. Once you have learned to square up and cross smoothly, however, you should work toward proofing against handling mistakes by teaching your dog to finish the poles no matter what awkward or distracting movements you might make.

...**Your dog may have missed the last pole or two despite good handling** on your part. It is natural and expected that your dog will make a mistake when learning something new. On your next several attempts, position wire guides at the last three poles to pattern a successful performance. Then gradually remove the guides.

HOW TO PROGRESS

When you have mastered switching from handling the poles off the left to handling off the right, perform the mirror image of the exercise by starting the poles off your right (Figure 5-16). This variation is more difficult because the dog exits in a direction that is opposite the direction you want him to turn. You may need to use wire guides at first to help prevent him from skipping the last pole.

Practice crossing in front using both flexible and rigid poles and be sure to use both odd and even-numbered sets. Then, gradually increase the angle of approach from jump #1 to the weave poles.

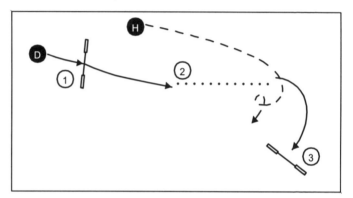

Figure 5-16: Cross-in-front side-switch from right to left.

Cross-Behind at Weave-Pole Entrance

When you can't get far enough ahead to cross in front of the weave poles, your best bet is to cross behind (Figure 5-17).

As when crossing behind on any other obstacle, the farther back you cross, the smoother your side-switch will be. Getting too close can interfere with your dog and cause him to balk at or miss the entry.

To ensure your dog's early success, use a set of only six weave poles to start your cross-behind training and position wire guides at poles #2 and #3. Begin as if you were completing a previous sequence off the right. Start parallel with your dog rather than leading out and start wide enough from him that you will not be taking a path into the wing of the first jump.

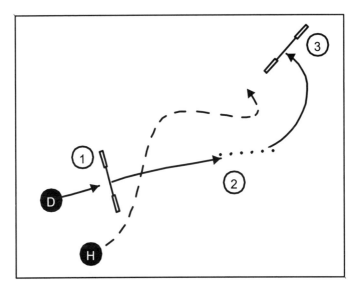

Figure 5-17: Cross-behind side-switch at entrance to weave poles.

Give your command and signal for jump #1. When your dog is in mid-air give your command for the weave poles while signaling with your left hand. As you move forward, use small, controlled steps to allow your dog to get ahead of you. Keep your shoulders firm and square with the weave poles as you smoothly move to the right behind him. When he has committed to the poles, smoothly and quickly take an extra step or two to your left so that you will be able to take a slightly converging path as your dog weaves. Resume your normal pace, keeping your shoulders facing slightly inward until the dog's nose crosses the last pole. Give your *Come!* command and turn left. Follow with your *Jump!* command when your dog's head has turned to see #3.

IF YOU HAVE PROBLEMS...

...Your dog may have been **reluctant to move ahead of you** to enter the weave poles. Go back to sending your dog through the weave poles using a target and wire guides. Resume your cross-behind training only after your dog can send through ahead without your crossing behind.

...Your dog may have **pulled out at or near the end of the weave poles.** Go wide and take a converging path after you have crossed the line of poles. Also make sure your shoulders are firmly turned slightly inward. Keeping your shoulders loose or turned outward may cause the dog to pull out.

Giving your dog this extra help with your body and handling path is good, conservative handling for occasions when it is possible to do so. Most likely, however, there will be some times that you do not handle this conservatively. Sometimes your handling may be rougher than planned. Other times you may want to pull away from the weave poles before your dog is finished to gain a strategic head start for the upcoming sequence. For these reasons, once you and your dog have mastered the cues for conservative handling, you will want to gradually proof your dog so that you know he will perform the complete set of poles regardless of any body movement you might make.

HOW TO PROGRESS

When you have mastered switching from handling the poles off the left to handling off the right, perform the mirror image of the exercise by starting the poles off your right (Figure 5-18). This variation is more difficult because the dog exits in a direction opposite the direction you want him to turn. You may need to use wire guides at first to help prevent him from skipping the last pole.

Gradually remove the wire guides and lengthen the set of the weave poles, making sure to practice with both odd- and even-numbered sets. Then, gradually increase the angle of approach from jump #1 to the weave poles.

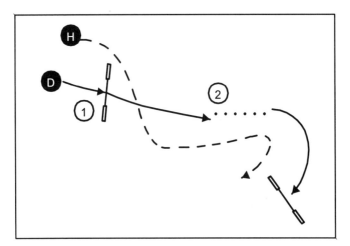

Figure 5-18: Cross-behind side-switch from right to left.

Things to Remember When Switching Sides

- With all of your side-switches, work to keep your movements smooth, controlled, and fluid. Giving jerky body motions or wildly flailing arms can draw the dog's attention to you instead of the obstacle ahead.

- If your dog is reluctant to move out ahead of you while you to cross behind him, go back to training your dog to send to each obstacle at a variety of angles and distances, as described in *Book 1: Obstacle Training*.

- When crossing in front of your dog, try to cross as far ahead of him as possible to avoid interfering with his movement. Any dog/handler contact that aids your dog's performance, whether intentional or not, can result in elimination on the course.

- When crossing behind your dog, cross as far back as possible to help ensure the smoothest side-switch possible. If at any time you get too close to the obstacle to smoothly cross behind, don't cross!

- Your choice of side-switch will be based on your prediction of where you will be in relation to your dog. If you can get far enough ahead, cross in front. The faster your dog is, the more likely you will need to handle the sequence preceding the cross-in-front at a distance. When getting ahead isn't your most competitive option, cross behind your dog.

- Avoid using the time-consuming pull-back side-switch whenever possible.

$\underline{6}$ The *Out!* Command

One of the most useful commands in agility is the *Out!* command. *Out!* means "turn away from the handler." For example, when you are handling off your left, saying *Come!* pulls the dog to his right, while saying *Out!* pushes the dog to his left.

Why use *Out!*

Some handlers use *Left!* and *Right!* commands for this purpose. These commands refer to the dog's left and right and are independent of the handler's position. Ideally, all dogs would master these commands. If they truly understood the concept, you could sit in a chair, sitting on your hands and direct your dog through an entire course! In reality, this is a very difficult goal for most dogs and handlers.

Most dogs follow body cues over verbal directions when the two conflict. Realistically, it takes a highly verbal dog and a continuous training effort to teach and maintain bona fide *Right!* and *Left!* commands.

What's more, even if the dog truly understands left and right, the handler is often a limiting factor. When the dog does something unexpected in the ring, the handler must decide immediately and under pressure whether the dog should turn to his right or his left and give the appropriate command in an instant. As a result, many right and left commands are given too late to do the job. If you are like most handlers, you may find it more practical to use *Come!*

and *Out!* than *Left!* and *Right!* Besides being easier to train, *Come!* and *Out!* are much more intuitive, so you are likely to give the correct command at the right time.

Handler Positions and the *Out!* Command

Consider the arrangement of obstacles in Figure 6-1.

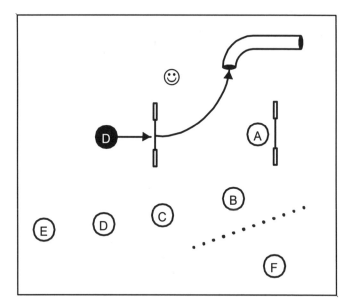

Figure 6-1: Handler positions for training the Out! command.

If you were handling your dog off your left, you would use an *Out!* command when the dog is in mid-air over the jump to turn him to the left toward the tunnel. If this situation were part of a course, your position during this maneuver could be just about anywhere. If this were the start of the course, you would be able to position yourself ahead of the dog at position A. This would clearly eliminate the jump

behind you as an option and would allow you to signal the
turn to the tunnel very clearly.

If the turn were later in the course, your position would be
dictated by where you were able to be when the dog
needed to make the turn. Sometimes you might be able to
be slightly ahead, but not directly in front of the dog, such
as at position B. Other times you may find yourself even
with the jump (C). Still other times you may find yourself either slightly behind (D) or significantly behind the jump (E)
when your dog is in mid-air. Alternatively, you may find
yourself handling wide and at a significant parallel distance
— with perhaps even an obstacle or two between you and
the dog (F) as he makes his turn. You can handle all of these
situations successfully using the *Out!* command. Regardless
of where you happen to be when you give your *Out!*
command, you will concurrently press toward the dog's intended path (indicated by the smiley face in Figure 6-1)
with your body and the palm of your signaling hand (the
hand closest to the dog).

To train a reliable *Out!* from a variety of positions, especially from behind the dog, can take weeks of training. The
investment in time, however, is well worth the effort.

How to Begin

In our first *Out!* training exercise, you will start in a clear
position ahead of the dog. As the dog catches on, you can
gradually lead out less and less, until your command will
work when you are only slightly ahead of him, alongside
him, then eventually behind him. You will also work on
gradually increasing your parallel distance from your dog.

Remember, we said that agility training is teaching your
dog, "When I do this, you do that"? With your *Out!* training
you will be building important verbal and physical cues that
will mean the same thing to your dog each time you use
them. This exercise will help you show the dog the differ-

ence between the cue for continuing straight ahead versus the cue for making a turn away from you.

To begin, arrange two jumps and a tunnel as shown in Figure 6-2. This is a new skill so the jumps should be set low. You are teaching a new command by association so you will want to do everything you can to help your dog get it right. Position a path marker to use as a push-point landmark at the position mid-way between the first jump and the tunnel opening (indicated by the smiley face).

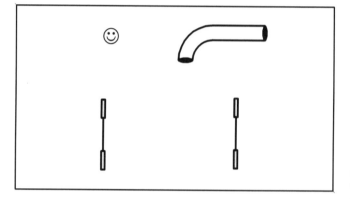

Figure 6-2: Setup for training the Out! command.

Position your dog squarely in front of the first jump and lead out as shown in Figure 6-3. Command him to jump. When he is in mid-air, give a clear *Out!* command and signal (flat palm of your left hand extended, fingers pointing upward) as you move toward a point between the tunnel and the first jump. Use small controlled steps and be sure to look at and move toward the marker — not the tunnel itself! When the dog's head has turned and can see the tunnel, give your *Tunnel!* command.

TRAINING TIP: *Your goal is to teach your dog what Out! means by association, therefore it is important that you say Out! (or whatever command you choose) clearly and enthusiastically — don't mumble or sound tentative.*

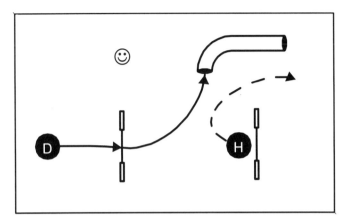

Figure 6-3: Begin your Out! training by starting directly in front of your dog.

If You Have Problems

…Your dog may have **bypassed the jump**. This can happen if you start moving or turn your shoulders before your dog is in mid-air over the jump. This practice of "jumping the gun" is particularly dangerous when you are working with wingless jumps. To avoid this problem, make an effort to remain square with the dog until he has taken off for the jump.

…Your dog may have **been reluctant to jump toward you** on your first command. This may happen if you bend or press forward toward your dog as you give your jump command. Some dogs may interpret this as a directive to stay. If this happens, relieve pressure on your dog by re-maining upright, or by taking a step or two backwards while giving your command to jump. Remember to keep square to the dog while pulling backward or you may cause your dog to run around the jump.

…**Your dog may not have turned toward the tunnel.** If your dog bypasses the tunnel, freeze and look at your feet. They should be facing the path marker. If you **face the tun-**

nel rather than the path, or if **you turn your shoulders too soon**, you could draw your dog away from the tunnel. With a dog that is slow to turn, keep walking toward your push-point landmark and don't waver from the path until your dog commits to the tunnel. When your dog is first learning this cue, you may have to take several steps toward the marker — perhaps even walk all the way to it. As your dog catches on, you will need to take fewer and fewer steps until all that will be necessary is your verbal command accompanied by a single step with forward pressure toward the path — regardless of how far away you are from your dog.

If your dog bypassed the tunnel despite perfect handling on your part, place him in a sit on the landing side of the jump and work on your push to the tunnel without the jump (Figure 6-4). It can be helpful to channel the dog to the tunnel using wire guides. Follow with an extra special reward for achieving success.

For the most difficult cases, it may help to show the dog a food-loaded target or toy placed after the tunnel. On the next try, the dog will most likely turn correctly to the tunnel, regardless of your handling. Don't use this as an excuse to handle poorly! Now that the dog is patterned for the behavior you want, your job is to handle correctly, so that you will couple the correct behavior with the cue you will use to get it on the agility course.

TRAINING TIP: In the early stages of this exercise, you may be tempted to run up toward the tunnel to show the dog where to go, rather than press toward the dog's path. Although your dog will most likely perform the tunnel when you do this — don't, as it eliminates the cue you are trying to train. You are attempting to train a cue that will work regardless of how close you are to the tunnel. Once you get any distance from the dog, your cue of heading toward the tunnel will not work. Pressing to the path <u>will</u> work at a distance and from a wide variety of handling positions.

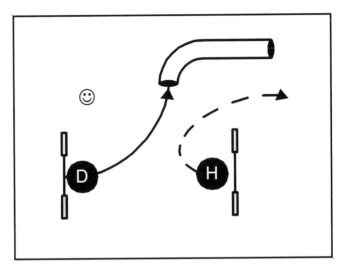

Figure 6-4: For dogs that have trouble, start in front of the jump.

How to Progress

Once you are successful using *Out!* from a position directly ahead of the dog, begin moving your starting position to make the exercise more difficult for him.

Presenting the Dog with Options

Gradually move your starting position to the side, as shown in Figure 6-5. Notice that the second jump is now visible and presents itself as an option to the dog.

> **NOTE:** *Different dogs will progress at vastly different rates when learning to respond to the Out! command. Some may progress to this level or even beyond during their first Out! training session. Others may need extra sessions at the initial starting position before their handlers begin making the exercise more difficult.*

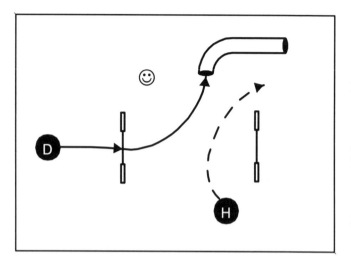

Figure 6-5: Work the Out! command from a position ahead of and to the side of the dog.

Out! vs. Straight Ahead

Before progressing too much further, it's time to emphasize to your dog the difference between the cue you will use to ask him to continue ahead versus the cue you will use to ask him to turn away from you.

Set your dog up and direct him over the two jumps, as shown in Figure 6-6. Since the dog is catching up to the back of you, your body will be facing parallel to the path you want him to take. This is a markedly different body cue from the one you will use to turn him away from you.

When your dog is in mid-air over the first jump, give your *Jump!* command. Do not preface it with a *Come!* command, even if you are worried that your dog might take the tunnel because he is patterned to do so. You are attempting to teach your dog the cues for each of the two options — straight ahead or outward turn. You should never use a *Come!* command between two jumps in a straight-line sequence, so it would be counterproductive and confuse the issue if you used it here.

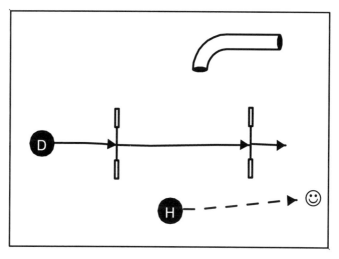

Figure 6-6: After patterning the Out! command, direct your dog to perform the two jumps.

Since your dog is patterned to take the tunnel, he may very well ignore your cue to jump. If this happens, give your non-emotional verbal correction (such as *Uh Oh!*, *Oops!*, or *Wrong!*). For your next attempt, physically block the tunnel with a wire guide or other barrier to make it easier to be successful. Alternatively, you could hold a toy in your signaling hand and throw it over the second jump as you give your command. Give a jackpot reward for success.

Once you get a successful two-jump sequence, ask for an *Out!* on the next try. When you can get the performance you want each time on your first try, you will know that your dog understands the cues you have taught him.

Decreasing Your Lead-Out

As you progress in your *Out!* training, gradually reduce your lead-out until you are even with the first jump, shown by handler position H1 in Figure 6-7. If you are successful, randomly alternate between the two-jump sequence and the jump-out-tunnel sequence.

When your dog can perform the sequence of your choice on your first attempt, it is time to start reducing your lead-out further until you are behind the dog (handler positions H2 and H3). Starting behind your dog can be difficult, therefore, in the beginning it is helpful to remove the second jump to help ensure success.

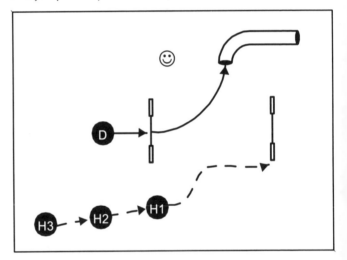

Figure 6-7: Gradually reduce your lead-out until you are starting behind your dog.

When working from behind the dog, give your *Out!* command coupled with a sharp shoulder turn, pressing toward the path marker — not toward the tunnel. For your signal, using the hand closest to the dog provides continuity so he is likely to respond quickly. It is consistent with the set of cues you have developed with your dog, so you are likely to avoid confusion or the dog looking up at you.

> **TRAINING TIP**: *Some people prefer to use the opposite hand for the Out! signal because it forces them to turn shoulders inward. If using the opposite hand feels better to you, and your dog understands you, go ahead and use it. Be aware, however, of the possible negative consequences. Your dog may interpret your change of signaling hands to indicate you are now working in the opposite direction. The farther you are away from your dog, the greater the likelihood of this misinterpretation. Moreover, the lack of continuity caused by switching hands may cause him to look up at you momentarily. This can sometimes result in a less-than-smooth performance.*

When you are successful, replace the second jump, but do not replace the jump bar. Once the dog is successful without the bar in place, replace it and repeat the exercise.

Randomly alternate between doing the two jumps and doing the jump-out-tunnel sequence. When you get the right behavior each time, you'll know you have taught the dog what you intended.

Working Without Body Cues

When you are successful from behind using your commands coupled with body cues, you may want to try repeating the exercise using verbal commands alone. At a trial, you will, of course, use both commands and body cues to communicate with your dog. Your body movements, however, have a lesser impact on your dog as you get farther away from him. For those cases, you will want your dog to fully understand and act upon hearing your verbal commands. To ensure he is listening and understands these commands, position yourself in the starting position and remain there for the entire exercise. Command jump-out-tunnel versus jump-jump (Figures 6-8 and 6-9). Make sure your command is absolutely on time, clear, and enthusiastic. When your dog can do each variation correctly on your verbal commands alone, you will be confident that your *Out!* command will work even when you are at a great distance from your dog.

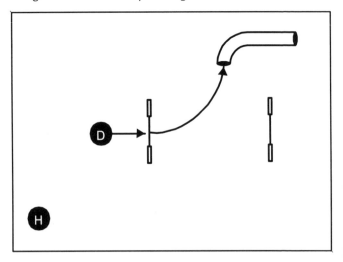

Figure 6-8: Using Out! from behind the dog on a verbal command alone.

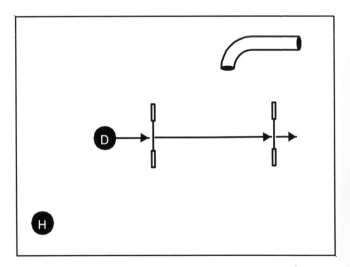

Figure 6-9: Directing the two-jump sequence from behind the dog on a verbal command alone.

Increasing Your Parallel Distance

Progress by gradually increasing your parallel distance from your dog, as shown in Figure 6-10.

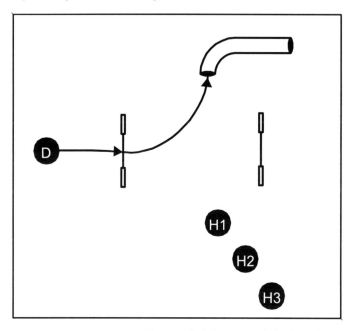

Figure 6-10: Increasing the parallel distance of the handler from the dog.

Eventually add obstacles between you and the dog as he is performing the *Out!* maneuver (Figure 6-11).

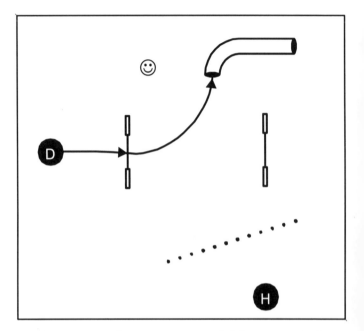

Figure 6-11: Working Out! at a parallel distance with obstacle layering.

Adding Speed

Getting an immediate turn using the *Out!* command becomes progressively harder as the dog's speed increases. For this reason, once you and your dog are comfortable with the exercise using one jump before the push to the tunnel, gradually add additional jumps to the beginning of the sequence (Figure 6-12). Start by leading out to place yourself in the most advantageous position for the turn (H1), then gradually reduce your lead-out until you are starting even with the dog (H5). Reducing your lead-out will simulate the times on the course when you are not able to get ahead of the dog.

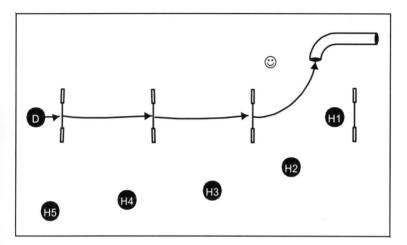

Figure 6-12: Adding speed by adding jumps. The handler gradually takes less and less of a lead-out.

Other Sequences Using *Out!*

Once your dog has caught on to the *Out!* command, you can begin to use it in a variety of sequences. The following pages contain examples of sequences incorporating *Out!* In all exercises, begin by leading out to the most advantageous position. When you are successful, begin to decrease your lead-out gradually. (For many exercises, you will probably want to increase your parallel distance from your dog as you reduce your lead-out.) This will simulate situations in which the sequence occurs within the body of a course, when you cannot position yourself in an optimum lead-out position for the sequence.

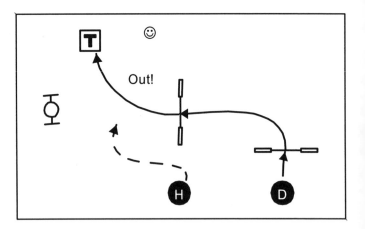

Out!

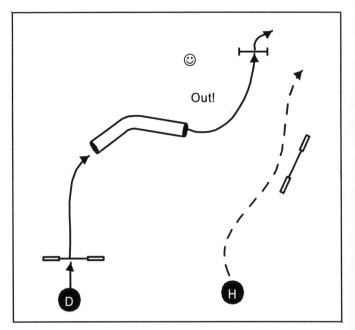

Out!

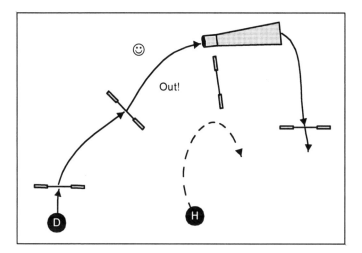

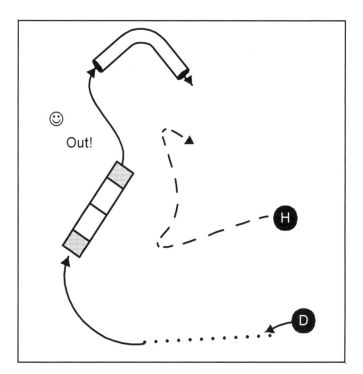

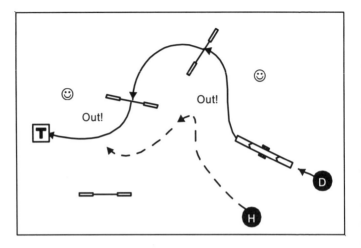

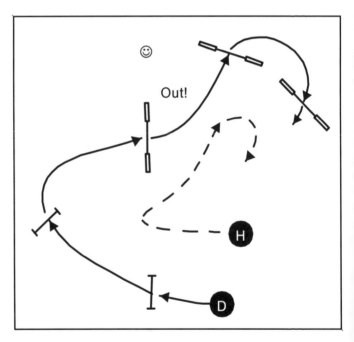

<u>7</u> The Distance Circle

D istance circles are great fun for your dog while they encourage him to look ahead and work away from you.

How to Begin

Start with a small circle of jumps and tunnels, as shown in Figure 7-1. First, pattern your dog to complete the circle in either direction.

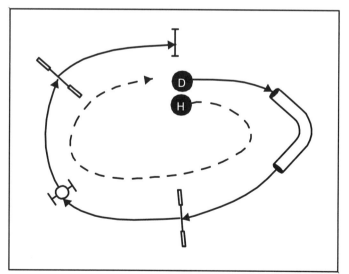

Figure 7-1: Pattern the circle to familiarize the dog with the sequence.

Once patterned, gradually increase your parallel distance until you are eventually occupying only a small circle in the center (Figure 7-2).

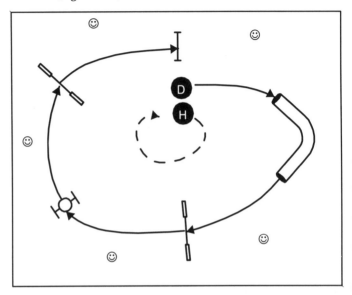

Figure 7-2: Gradually increase your parallel distance until you are handling from a small circle in the center.

You can begin the exercise from your side on the fly, as shown in Figures 7-1 and 7-2, or from an offset start position, as shown in Figure 7-3.

It's easiest to start with the tunnel. As soon as your dog enters, you can back up to position yourself closer to the center of the circle. When your dog exits the tunnel, you can then press outward toward the path with your left hand to direct him over the jump. The path markers are indicated in the exercise diagrams by smiley faces ☺. At any given point in the sequence, you want to be facing between where the dog is and where you want him to go. For example, when he leaves the tunnel you want to be facing between the tunnel exit and the next jump, while giving your *Jump!* command.

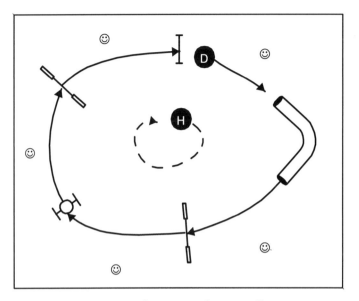

Figure 7-3: Beginning the exercise from an offset start.

Many handlers trying this exercise for the first time will have a tendency to take a step toward the path marker and freeze. You will have much better results if you keep moving, even if you are only taking small steps. Dogs have excellent peripheral vision and they can see and sense your movement even when you are behind them.

When you stop moving, you are no longer giving information to your dog. And a result, he may stop or lose momentum, and check back with you. As you are moving, remember to keep your shoulders and flat-palm signal square to the path markers between each obstacle. From the dog's point of view, this makes it clear where you want him to go.

If You Have Problems

...Your dog may have **run past an obstacle** (Figure 7-4). This may happen if you face the next obstacle rather than the desired path. From the dog's point of view, it appears that you want him to skip the next obstacle. Try the exercise again, this time making an effort to face the path, rather than the obstacle.

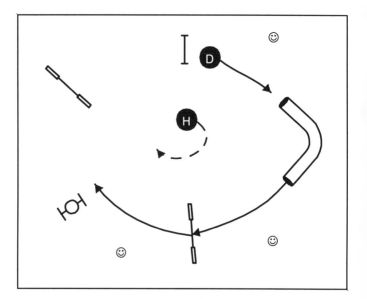

Figure 7-4: Facing the tire, rather than facing the point between the jump and the tire, causes a runout.

This may also happen if you **run in too close** to the obstacles and then start to **pull away**. If your dog bypasses an obstacle and you're not sure of the reason, freeze and look at your feet. Are they facing the path — between the dog's current position and the next obstacle you want him to take? Chances are they are facing either the obstacle, or even a point past the obstacle. If you're still not sure, blame your dog last.

What your dog sees when you face the entrance to the tunnel, rather than the path. Can you tell for certain which end is correct?

What your dog sees when you face the path to the tunnel entrance. Is the correct end clearer now?

How to Progress

Practice the exercise in both directions. Then start inserting some random call-offs. You may also want to throw in some random "agains" (as described in *Chapter1: Obedience, Directional, and Control Commands*). *Again!* is a command that means take the obstacle you last performed in the opposite direction. It is useful in the game of Gamblers, as well as an instructional tool for your training sessions.

Once you have patterned a sequence, you can use the *Again!* command to surprise your dog with a change of direction (Figure 7-5). This helps teach him to listen closely to your commands rather than to operate on autopilot. It also helps keep training interesting and fun for both you and your canine partner.

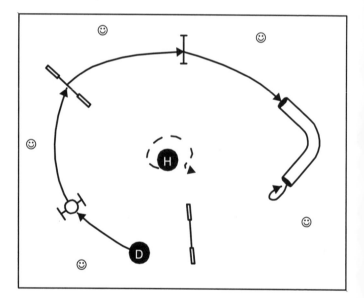

Figure 7-5: Using the Again! command to surprise your dog with a change of direction.

Once you have mastered sequencing on this circle, gradually increase its size. Then add more difficult obstacles, such as contacts and weave poles (Figure 7-6). You can use wire guides with the weave poles and contact obstacles to prevent your dog from making mistakes while you are working on increasing distance.

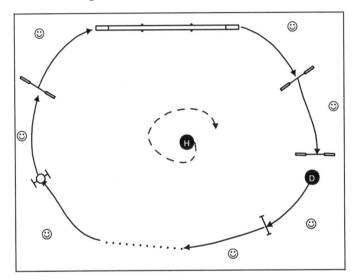

Figure 7-6: Progress to incorporating weave poles and contact obstacles in your distance circles.

8 Mastering Longer Sequences

When your dog has mastered three- and four-obstacle sequences with side-switches, you are ready to try five- and six-obstacle sequences — and then even longer ones. You will gradually be building your dog's ability to chain more behaviors together, while you increase your ability to maintain your concentration at the same time.

Progress gradually, one obstacle at a time, adding obstacles only when the previous sequence is perfect. Short stretches of excellence greatly outweigh long stretches of mediocrity.

Include a variety of jumps in your sequences such as wingless, spread jumps, and decorative jumps — all set at a variety of non-challenging heights.

When including weave poles in your sequences, using training poles and/or wire guides is often a good idea to ensure early success. Doing so makes it likely that your dog will complete the weave poles quickly and accurately. This leaves you free to concentrate on teaching your dog (and yourself) to smoothly navigate through progressively longer and more complex sequences.

You can further ensure success if you first position weave poles after control obstacles such as the pause table or contact obstacles. When your dog is more experienced you can then place the weave poles after speed obstacles such as jumps and tunnels.

Dealing with Mistakes

As your sequences become longer, you will no doubt encounter some problems. Resist the urge to continue when a mistake is made! If your dog makes a mistake between obstacles #3 and #4, stop. Try to determine the cause of the problem and make it more likely for your dog to succeed next time. Then, start with obstacle #3 and if successful, end with #4. Follow with lavish praise and a sizable reward.

By stopping immediately and working through the problem, you can isolate and reward the skill that you and your dog had trouble with. If you were to continue after achieving success instead of stopping to reward, your dog could easily make a mistake on obstacle #5 or #6. You would then miss an opportunity to reward your dog for the improvement from #3 to #4.

Likewise, after a mistake made between #3 and #4, don't start back with #1. Your dog could make a mistake before you get a chance to reward a successful attempt at #3 to #4.

Missing an opportunity to tell a dog he's on the right track is one of the biggest mistakes a dog trainer can make. Sometimes this is one of the hardest concepts to get across to students. During a stellar or much improved performance, students often get on a roll and are reluctant to quit while they are ahead.

Every time you isolate and reward an improved performance of a skill, you strengthen it and make it more likely to happen again in the future. If you were to ignore the improvement, your dog is likely to try something totally different the next time in an effort to win your approval.

Sample Sequences

The following pages contain sample sequences, starting with 5-obstacle sequences and progressing to 10-obstacle sequences. When adding length, it's a good idea to **back-chain**, that is, to start with the last few obstacles. Then, if successful, gradually add obstacles to the beginning of the sequence. In this way, the dog is always progressing from the unfamiliar to the familiar and is more likely to achieve success.

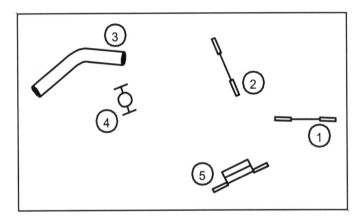

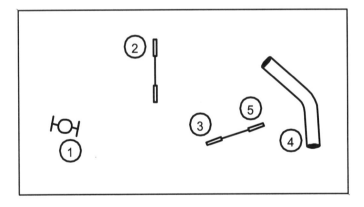

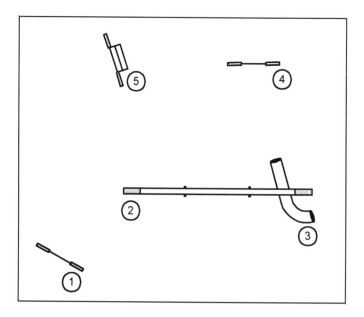

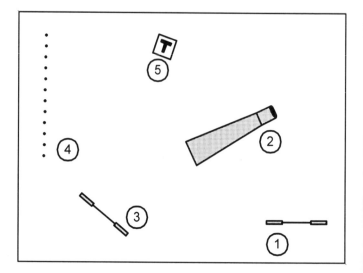

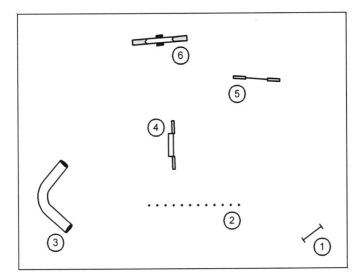

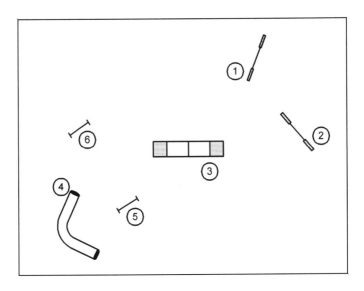

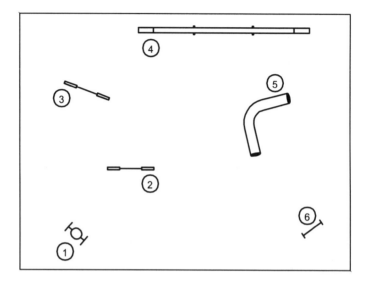

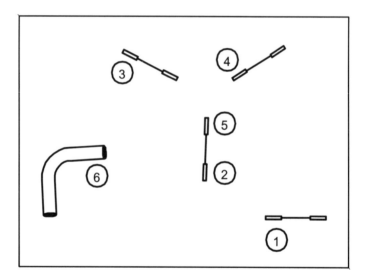

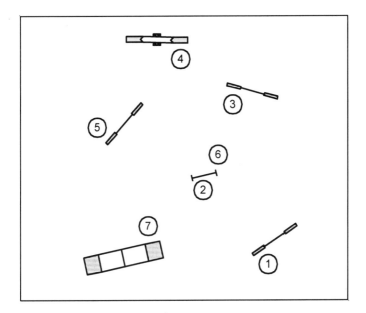

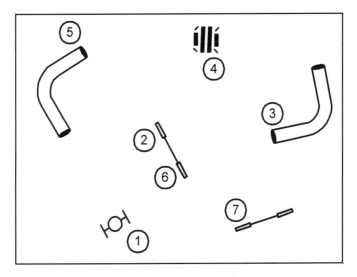

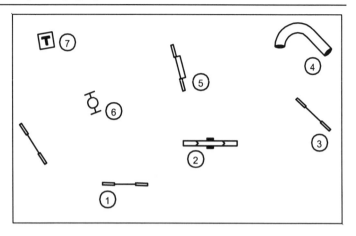

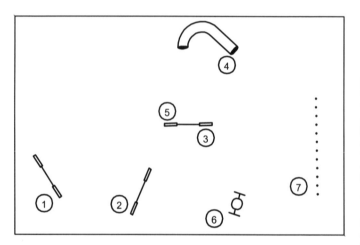

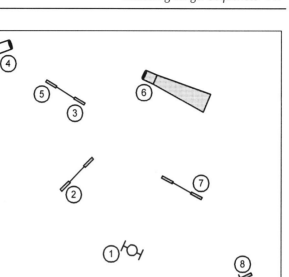

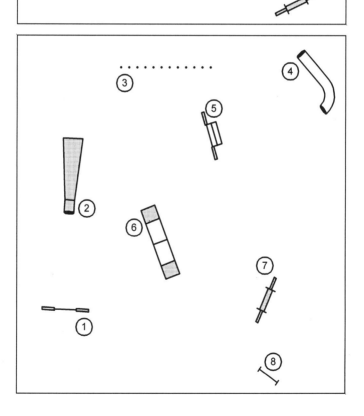

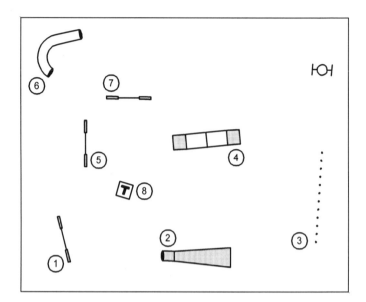

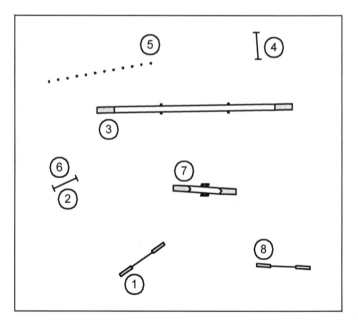

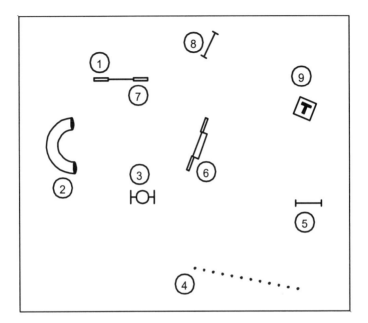

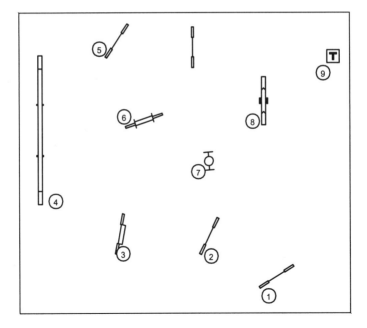

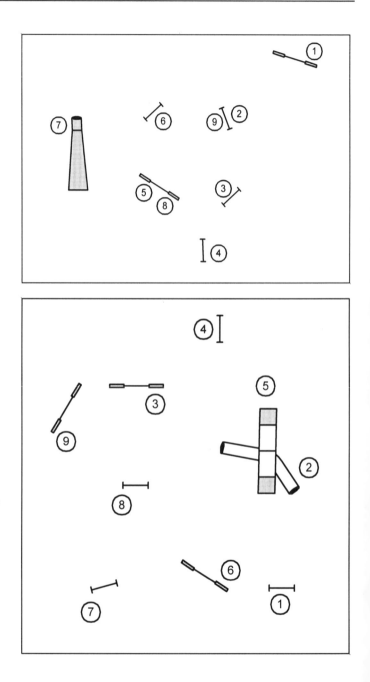

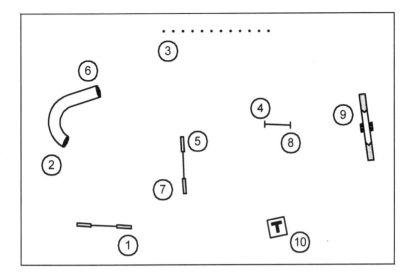

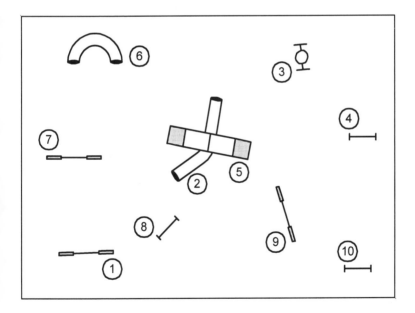

Developing reliability on the weave poles through proofing.

9 Developing Reliability

Have you ever heard any of your agility friends moan, when things go awry on the agility course: "but he does it *perfectly* at home!" Perhaps you've even uttered this all-too-common phrase yourself on more than one occasion. Unfortunately, it's unlikely that the next agility trial will be held in the familiar sanctuary of your backyard. Many trials are held in busy parks, complete with softball practice or family picnics right outside the ring. Sometimes your dog will be required to compete in the rain, or on agility obstacles that look very different from what your dog is accustomed to. Moreover, many trials are held in dirt-floored livestock arenas, complete with birds in the rafters and a delightful array of dog-attracting scents.

If you've followed the program outlined in *Excelling at Dog Agility — Book 1: Obstacle Training,* you have already begun developing reliability through *proofing.* Just as it was with your obstacle training, proofing is an essential part of your dog's sequence training that teaches your dog to perform with focus, speed, and accuracy under a wide variety of conditions. Proofing solidifies a dog's understanding of an exercise, while strengthening his concentration and confidence. As a result of proofing, you will most likely find that your runs are both faster and more accurate. Moreover, because proofing injects novelty and challenge into your training sessions, your dog is much less likely to become bored with his training.

Proofing gives both you and your dog the confidence to do your best, and to relax and have fun at the same time. If you choose to omit this all-important process, you may be forced to resort to the ulcer-causing practice known as "cross your fingers and pray." Because you are unsure about how your dog will perform, you will most likely be nervous in the competition ring. This can easily prevent you from handling smoothly and with confidence. What's more, your nervousness will be transmitted to the dog, which can affect his performance as well.

Begin proofing *only after your dog has thoroughly learned an exercise.* This means that your dog will quickly and accurately perform the exercise every time on your first command and/or signal in familiar settings. It usually requires several weeks of work to reach this level, depending on the behavior you are training.

The following principles should apply to all of your proofing work:

- Use extra-special rewards when proofing such as people-food treats or toys that your dog doesn't receive in your regular training sessions.

- Start slowly and gradually increase the intensity of your proofing. Different dogs will be able to handle vastly different rates of escalation. If you notice any signs of stress — ears pinned back, lip licking, or disinterest in food — you are progressing too quickly.

- When your dog makes a mistake, don't repeat your command. Instead, mark the moment of the error with a non-emotional verbal correction such as *Uh Oh!*, *Oops!* or *Wrong!* Then back off slightly on the level of proofing and help the dog be correct on the next try. It may help to have your dog wear a short, leather grab tab and a tight-fitting buckle collar, so that you can give him a motivational launch in the correct direction, followed by enthusiastic praise. Reward profusely when your dog achieves success!

Begin with a few mild distractions.

Eventually progress to a variety of stronger distractions.

Your proofing program should desensitize your dog to a wide variety of sights, sounds, and tempting distractions. Start your proofing with obedience commands and individual obstacles, then progress to sequences. Begin by working close to your dog and then gradually add distance.

Practice the *Sit!* and *Down!* commands on a variety of surfaces. Start with pleasant, familiar surfaces then progress to more difficult ones such as wet grass, mud, pine needles and gravel. Proof your *Stay!* or *Wait!* command by throwing toys or food containers, cheering, and running away from your dog. You can also attach a lead and apply mild pressure to reinforce the concept of waiting. Always reward when your dog is in the correct position – never reward the release. Practice recalls with tempting alternatives to coming, such as enticing rewards or obstacles just ahead.

To prepare your dog for competition obstacles that look different from those at home, try to expose him to a variety of equipment. If you are one of the many people, however, who train in an area with limited access to obstacles, you can accomplish the same goal by making your own equipment look and feel unfamiliar to your dog.

- Hang scarves, feather boas, sheets, balloons, or other distracting objects over jump bars, wings, and tunnels.

- For the seesaw, varied pivot points and unfamiliar noise present a problem to many new agility dogs. Secure weights to various places on the seesaw plank to give your dog experience with a variety of pivot points. Place a metal cookie sheet under the downside to help simulate the distracting noise that some seesaws make.

- Change the look and feel of your pause table by attaching temporary surfaces. Add-on materials that work well include sheets of corrugated plastic or cardboard, or fabric such as towels, sheets, and blankets.

- Practice occasionally with wet pause tables and wet closed-tunnel chutes.

- Make your weave poles appear different by using colored tape. To make them less visible, tape your weave poles a solid dark color, or tape alternating poles in different colors for an additional challenge. Practice with odd- and even-numbered sets, and work occasionally with more than 12 poles.

Teach your dog to tune-out distracting conditions by being fun and inventive. It doesn't matter if the distractions you use are unlikely to be present at an agility trial. Your work at ignoring distractions of any kind will carry over to the agility ring. Try some of the following:

- Ask friends to clap and cheer, rattle treat bags, toss balls back and forth to one another, and squeak vinyl toys from the sidelines or from within the ring.

- Play music, sound-effects tapes, and dog-show-noise tapes while you are working.

- Place people and friendly dogs next to the obstacles. Start with stationary distractions, and then progress to moving ones.

- Position pinwheels, mechanical toys, and other moving objects within the training area.

- Place enticing objects on the ground between obstacles. You can use sealed dog-treat containers, toys, even an old loaf of bread with holes poked in the bag. It is important that the dog not be able to reward himself if he investigates the distraction, so make sure the food containers are sealed and that the toys are protected by you or a training partner.

Eventually you can run an entire practice course with a variety of distractions. Most dogs will really enjoy the challenge. What's more, your hard work will reward you with a faster, more focused dog that actively works to concentrate on your directives.

The care you have taken to provide a thoughtful and systematic foundation in sequencing will repay you many times over in the months and years ahead. (Photo: Tien Tran Photography)

10 Where to Go From Here

By now you have learned to sequence smoothly and confidently from one obstacle to the next. You have also mastered turns and side-switches, and your dog has developed reliability under a variety of conditions. The care you have taken to provide a thoughtful and systematic foundation in sequencing will repay you many times over in the months and years ahead. What's more, you have continued to develop a happy working relationship with your dog based on trust, consistency, mutual respect, and high expectations.

If any of the concepts presented in this book have not been clear to you, it may help to review the appropriate sections in the corresponding video, *Competitive Agility Training with Jane Simmons-Moake — Tape 2: Sequence Training*. To help you locate specific topics, a *Video Topic Guide* is provided in *Appendix B*.

Once you have mastered all of the skills in *Book 2: Sequence Training*, you are ready to progress to *Excelling at Dog Agility — Book 3: Advanced Skills Training*. Through *Book 3*, you will develop additional high-level skills that, once mastered, can offer you great flexibility in how you choose to handle a course. With each new skill you master, you will gain a competitive edge by shaving off seconds and increasing your available handling options. At the same time, agility training will become even more fun and challenging for both you and your canine companion.

(Photo: Tien Tran Photography)

Appendix A: Sample Lesson Plans for Group Instruction

Although individual instruction is optimal in that it allows you the freedom to proceed at the pace most suited to your dog, most people must rely on group instruction for their agility training. Besides being practical and affordable, group classes allow you to train in a fun atmosphere, where you will meet other people who share your enthusiasm for the sport. Moreover, group classes provide a distracting environment for your dog. This may make training more challenging at first; however, it will eventually reward you with a dog who is accustomed to working around other dogs and people – much like the environment you will be competing in at an agility trial.

The following pages contain sample lesson plans for a six-week Beginning Agility course, an eight-week Intermediate I Agility course, and a six-week Intermediate II Agility course. These plans are included in this book to give you some ideas for designing your own group instruction.

The sample lesson plans are for hour-long classes of 14-16 students with two instructors and two assistants. Your available agility equipment, working area, and instructional staff will play a large role in how many students you can safely and effectively teach, and the required length of your class sessions. If your working area is small, or if you have a limited supply of agility equipment, or if the size of your instructional staff is small, you may need to accept a smaller number of students or plan for the classes to run longer.

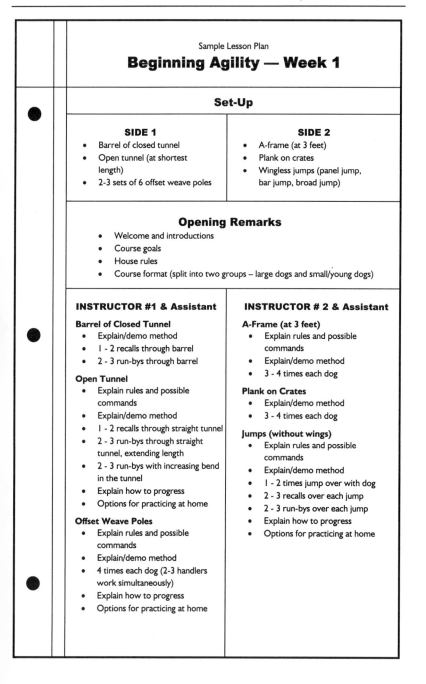

Sample Lesson Plan

Beginning Agility — Week 1

Set-Up

SIDE 1

- Barrel of closed tunnel
- Open tunnel (at shortest length)
- 2-3 sets of 6 offset weave poles

SIDE 2

- A-frame (at 3 feet)
- Plank on crates
- Wingless jumps (panel jump, bar jump, broad jump)

Opening Remarks

- Welcome and introductions
- Course goals
- House rules
- Course format (split into two groups – large dogs and small/young dogs)

INSTRUCTOR #1 & Assistant

Barrel of Closed Tunnel
- Explain/demo method
- 1 - 2 recalls through barrel
- 2 - 3 run-bys through barrel

Open Tunnel
- Explain rules and possible commands
- Explain/demo method
- 1 - 2 recalls through straight tunnel
- 2 - 3 run-bys through straight tunnel, extending length
- 2 - 3 run-bys with increasing bend in the tunnel
- Explain how to progress
- Options for practicing at home

Offset Weave Poles
- Explain rules and possible commands
- Explain/demo method
- 4 times each dog (2-3 handlers work simultaneously)
- Explain how to progress
- Options for practicing at home

INSTRUCTOR # 2 & Assistant

A-Frame (at 3 feet)
- Explain rules and possible commands
- Explain/demo method
- 3 - 4 times each dog

Plank on Crates
- Explain/demo method
- 3 - 4 times each dog

Jumps (without wings)
- Explain rules and possible commands
- Explain/demo method
- 1 - 2 times jump over with dog
- 2 - 3 recalls over each jump
- 2 - 3 run-bys over each jump
- Explain how to progress
- Options for practicing at home

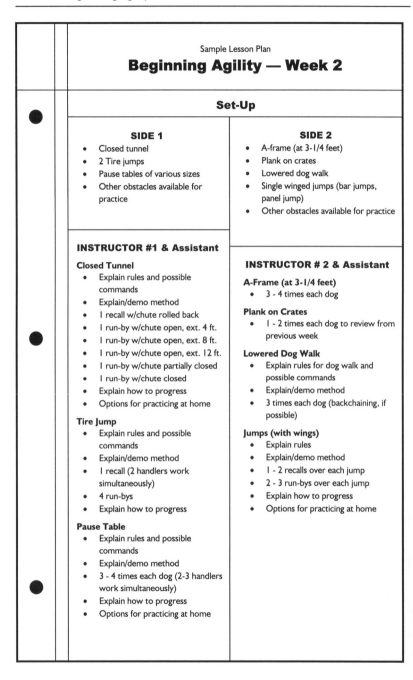

Sample Lesson Plan

Beginning Agility — Week 2

Set-Up

SIDE 1	SIDE 2
• Closed tunnel	• A-frame (at 3-1/4 feet)
• 2 Tire jumps	• Plank on crates
• Pause tables of various sizes	• Lowered dog walk
• Other obstacles available for practice	• Single winged jumps (bar jumps, panel jump)
	• Other obstacles available for practice

INSTRUCTOR #1 & Assistant

Closed Tunnel
- Explain rules and possible commands
- Explain/demo method
- I recall w/chute rolled back
- I run-by w/chute open, ext. 4 ft.
- I run-by w/chute open, ext. 8 ft.
- I run-by w/chute open, ext. 12 ft.
- I run-by w/chute partially closed
- I run-by w/chute closed
- Explain how to progress
- Options for practicing at home

Tire Jump
- Explain rules and possible commands
- Explain/demo method
- I recall (2 handlers work simultaneously)
- 4 run-bys
- Explain how to progress

Pause Table
- Explain rules and possible commands
- Explain/demo method
- 3 - 4 times each dog (2-3 handlers work simultaneously)
- Explain how to progress
- Options for practicing at home

INSTRUCTOR # 2 & Assistant

A-Frame (at 3-1/4 feet)
- 3 - 4 times each dog

Plank on Crates
- I - 2 times each dog to review from previous week

Lowered Dog Walk
- Explain rules for dog walk and possible commands
- Explain/demo method
- 3 times each dog (backchaining, if possible)

Jumps (with wings)
- Explain rules
- Explain/demo method
- I - 2 recalls over each jump
- 2 - 3 run-bys over each jump
- Explain how to progress
- Options for practicing at home

Sample Lesson Plan
Beginning Agility — Week 3

Set-Up

SIDE 1	SIDE 2
• 2 Tire jumps	• A-frame (at 3-1/2 feet)
• Closed tunnel	• Lowered dog walk
• 2-3 sets of 6 offset weave poles	• Spread jumps: double- and triple-bar
• Other obstacles available for practice	• Other obstacles available for practice

INSTRUCTOR #1 & Assistant

Tire Jump
- Review run-bys
- 3 - 4 times each dog (2 handlers work simultaneously)

Closed Tunnel
- Review run-bys starting w/fully open and extended, progressing to closed
- 3 - 4 times each dog

Offset Weave Poles
- Review method
- 3 - 4 times each dog (2-3 handlers work simultaneously)

INSTRUCTOR # 2 & Assistant

A-Frame (at 3-1/2 feet)
- Review method
- 3 - 4 times each dog

Lowered Dog Walk
- Review method
- 3 times each dog

Double- and Triple-Bar Spread Jumps
- Explain/demo method
- 1 - 2 recalls over each jump
- 2 - 3 run-bys over each jump

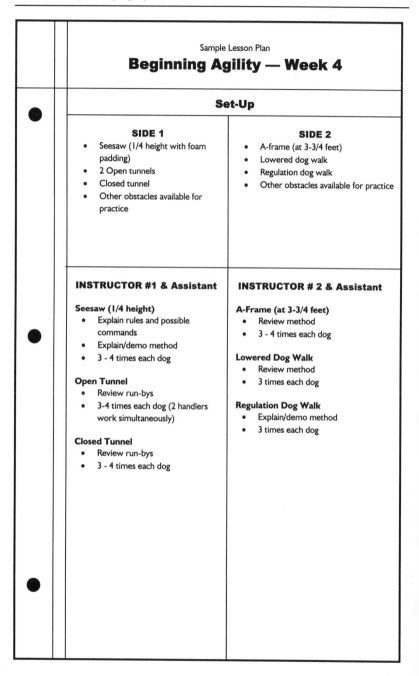

Sample Lesson Plan

Beginning Agility — Week 4

Set-Up

SIDE 1	SIDE 2
• Seesaw (1/4 height with foam padding) • 2 Open tunnels • Closed tunnel • Other obstacles available for practice	• A-frame (at 3-3/4 feet) • Lowered dog walk • Regulation dog walk • Other obstacles available for practice

INSTRUCTOR #1 & Assistant	INSTRUCTOR # 2 & Assistant
Seesaw (1/4 height) • Explain rules and possible commands • Explain/demo method • 3 - 4 times each dog **Open Tunnel** • Review run-bys • 3-4 times each dog (2 handlers work simultaneously) **Closed Tunnel** • Review run-bys • 3 - 4 times each dog	**A-Frame (at 3-3/4 feet)** • Review method • 3 - 4 times each dog **Lowered Dog Walk** • Review method • 3 times each dog **Regulation Dog Walk** • Explain/demo method • 3 times each dog

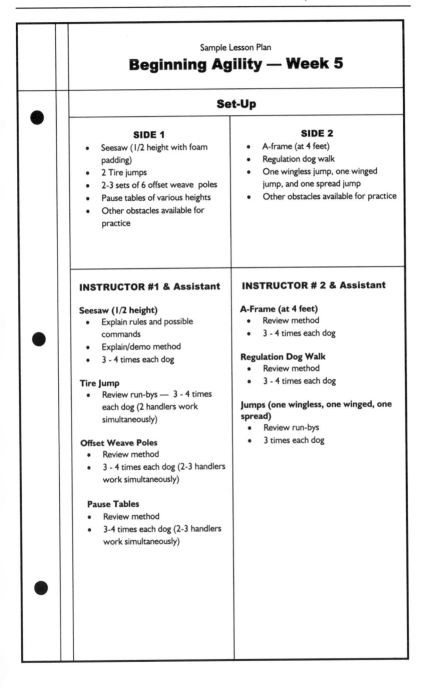

Sample Lesson Plan

Beginning Agility — Week 5

Set-Up

SIDE 1
- Seesaw (1/2 height with foam padding)
- 2 Tire jumps
- 2-3 sets of 6 offset weave poles
- Pause tables of various heights
- Other obstacles available for practice

SIDE 2
- A-frame (at 4 feet)
- Regulation dog walk
- One wingless jump, one winged jump, and one spread jump
- Other obstacles available for practice

INSTRUCTOR #1 & Assistant

Seesaw (1/2 height)
- Explain rules and possible commands
- Explain/demo method
- 3 - 4 times each dog

Tire Jump
- Review run-bys — 3 - 4 times each dog (2 handlers work simultaneously)

Offset Weave Poles
- Review method
- 3 - 4 times each dog (2-3 handlers work simultaneously)

Pause Tables
- Review method
- 3-4 times each dog (2-3 handlers work simultaneously)

INSTRUCTOR # 2 & Assistant

A-Frame (at 4 feet)
- Review method
- 3 - 4 times each dog

Regulation Dog Walk
- Review method
- 3 - 4 times each dog

Jumps (one wingless, one winged, one spread)
- Review run-bys
- 3 times each dog

Sample Lesson Plan

Beginning Agility — Week 6

Set-Up

- Arrange obstacles in a simple sequence.
- Set A-frame at 4-1/4 feet.
- Place number markers next to each obstacle.

INSTRUCTOR #1 & Assistant

Seesaw (1/2 height)
- Review method
- 3 - 4 times each dog

Closed Tunnel
- Review method
- 3 - 4 run-bys each dog

INSTRUCTOR # 2 & Assistant

A-Frame (at 4-1/4 feet)
- Review method
- 3 - 4 times each dog

Regulation Dog Walk
- Review method
- 3 - 4 times each dog

Putting it Together

- Each dog performs each obstacle at controlled pace.
- Students are not scored or timed — they are asked to focus on dog performing on one clear command and signal rather than speed.
- Instructors alternate accompanying handlers around the course to assist when needed.

Closing Remarks

- Distribute Certificates of Participation
- Options for continuing your training
- Obedience requirements for Intermediate and Advanced-level training

Sample Lesson Plan
Intermediate I Agility — Week 1

Set-Up

SIDE 1	SIDE 2
• 2 Open tunnels	• Dog walk
• 2 Pause tables	• 2 Winged jumps
• Seesaw (1/2 height w/ padding)	• A-frame (at 4-1/2 feet)
• Other obstacles available for practice	• Other obstacles available for practice

Opening Remarks
- Course goals
- House rules
- Course format (split into two groups – large dogs and small/young dogs)
- Introduction to sending and calling to individual obstacles

INSTRUCTOR #1 & Assistant

Calling/Sending to Open Tunnel
- Explain/demo method (2 dogs work simultaneously)
- Call via offset start at different angles, 2-3 times each dog
- Send on the fly to tunnel and target at different angles, 2-3 times each dog

Calling/Sending to Pause Table
- Explain/demo method (2 dogs work simultaneously)
- Call via offset start at different angles, 2-3 times each dog
- Send on the fly to tunnel and target at different angles, 2-3 times each dog

Seesaw (1/2 height – angled approaches for those who are ready)
- Review method
- 3-4 times each dog

INSTRUCTOR # 2 & Assistant

Calling/Sending to Dog Walk
- Explain/demo method
- Call via offset start at different angles, 2-3 times each dog
- Send on the fly to tunnel and target at different angles, 2-3 times each dog

Calling/Sending to Winged Jump
- Explain/demo method (2 dogs work simultaneously)
- Call via offset start at different angles, 2-3 times each dog
- Send on the fly to tunnel and target at different angles, 2-3 times each dog

A-frame at 4-1/2 feet
- Review method
- 3-4 times each dog

Sample Course Outline

Intermediate I Agility — Week 2

Set-Up

SIDE 1	SIDE 2
• 2 Closed tunnels	• A-frame (set at 4-1/2 feet)
• Pause tables of various heights	• 2 – 3 sets of 6 offset weave poles
• Seesaw (3/4 height with foam padding)	• Other obstacles available for practice
• Other obstacles available for practice	

INSTRUCTOR #1 & Assistant	**INSTRUCTOR # 2 & Assistant**
Calling/Sending to Closed Tunnel	**Calling/Sending to A-frame at 4-1/2 feet**
• Explain/demo method (2 dogs will work simultaneously)	• Explain/demo method
• Call via offset start at different angles, 2-3 times each dog	• Call via offset start at different angles, 2-3 times each dog
• Send on the fly to tunnel and target at different angles, 2-3 times each dog	• Send on the fly to A-frame and target at different angles, 2-3 times each dog
Calling/Sending to Tire Jump	**Calling Through Offset Weave Poles**
• Explain/demo method (2 dogs will work simultaneously)	• Explain/demo method (2-3 dogs will work simultaneously)
• Call via offset start at different angles, 2-3 times each dog	• 3-4 times each dog
• Send on the fly to tire jump and target at different angles, 2-3 times each dog	
Seesaw (3/4 height)	
• Review method	
• 3-4 times each dog	

Sample Lesson Plan

Intermediate I Agility — Week 3

Set-Up

Set up three 3-obstacle straight-line sequences on each instructor's side. Space obstacles 18 feet apart. Use as many different obstacles as possible to provide supervised practice. A-frame is at 4-1/2 feet, weave poles are sets of 6 offsets, see-saw is ¾ height. Any obstacles not used in the sequences should be set up and available for practice. At the end of class, each participant will have worked through six straight-line sequences. He will also have had an opportunity to practice individual obstacles before and after class and while awaiting his turn.

Opening Remarks

- Introduction to straight-line sequences and call-offs
- Keep it fun but concentrate on handling

INSTRUCTOR #1 & Assistant	**INSTRUCTOR #2 & Assistant**
3-Obstacle Straight-Line Sequence • Explain/demo method • Last two obstacles only, 1 time each dog • Entire 3-obstacle sequence, 2 times each dog	**3-Obstacle Straight-Line Sequence** • Explain/demo method • Last two obstacles only, 1 time each dog • Entire 3-obstacle sequence, 2 times each dog
3-Obstacle Straight-Line Sequence • Explain/demo method • Last two obstacles only, 1 time each dog • Entire 3-obstacle sequence, 2 times each dog	**3-Obstacle Straight-Line Sequence** • Explain/demo method • Last two obstacles only, 1 time each dog • Entire 3-obstacle sequence, 2 times each dog
3-Obstacle Straight-Line Sequence • Explain/demo method • Last two obstacles only, 1 time each dog • Entire 3-obstacle sequence, 2 times each dog • Call-off after 2nd obstacle, 1 time each dog	**3-Obstacle Straight-Line Sequence** • Explain/demo method • Last two obstacles only, 1 time each dog • Entire 3-obstacle sequence, 2 times each dog • Call-off after 2nd obstacle, 1 time each dog

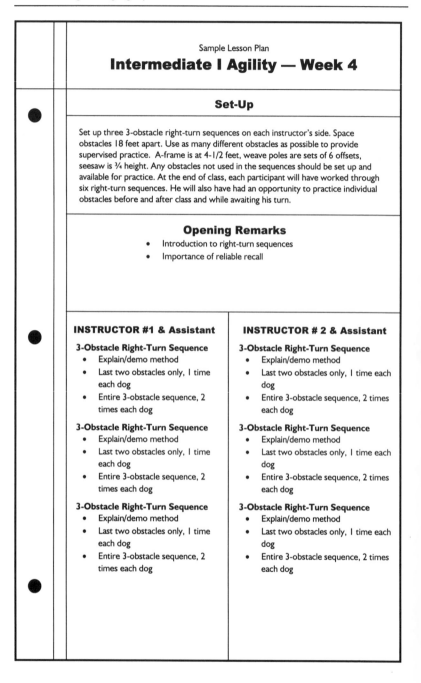

Sample Lesson Plan

Intermediate I Agility — Week 4

Set-Up

Set up three 3-obstacle right-turn sequences on each instructor's side. Space obstacles 18 feet apart. Use as many different obstacles as possible to provide supervised practice. A-frame is at 4-1/2 feet, weave poles are sets of 6 offsets, seesaw is ¾ height. Any obstacles not used in the sequences should be set up and available for practice. At the end of class, each participant will have worked through six right-turn sequences. He will also have had an opportunity to practice individual obstacles before and after class and while awaiting his turn.

Opening Remarks

- Introduction to right-turn sequences
- Importance of reliable recall

INSTRUCTOR #1 & Assistant

3-Obstacle Right-Turn Sequence
- Explain/demo method
- Last two obstacles only, 1 time each dog
- Entire 3-obstacle sequence, 2 times each dog

3-Obstacle Right-Turn Sequence
- Explain/demo method
- Last two obstacles only, 1 time each dog
- Entire 3-obstacle sequence, 2 times each dog

3-Obstacle Right-Turn Sequence
- Explain/demo method
- Last two obstacles only, 1 time each dog
- Entire 3-obstacle sequence, 2 times each dog

INSTRUCTOR # 2 & Assistant

3-Obstacle Right-Turn Sequence
- Explain/demo method
- Last two obstacles only, 1 time each dog
- Entire 3-obstacle sequence, 2 times each dog

3-Obstacle Right-Turn Sequence
- Explain/demo method
- Last two obstacles only, 1 time each dog
- Entire 3-obstacle sequence, 2 times each dog

3-Obstacle Right-Turn Sequence
- Explain/demo method
- Last two obstacles only, 1 time each dog
- Entire 3-obstacle sequence, 2 times each dog

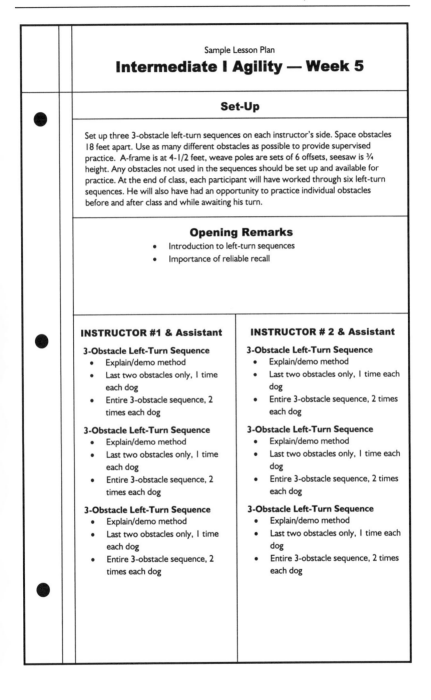

Sample Lesson Plan

Intermediate I Agility — Week 5

Set-Up

Set up three 3-obstacle left-turn sequences on each instructor's side. Space obstacles 18 feet apart. Use as many different obstacles as possible to provide supervised practice. A-frame is at 4-1/2 feet, weave poles are sets of 6 offsets, seesaw is ¾ height. Any obstacles not used in the sequences should be set up and available for practice. At the end of class, each participant will have worked through six left-turn sequences. He will also have had an opportunity to practice individual obstacles before and after class and while awaiting his turn.

Opening Remarks

- Introduction to left-turn sequences
- Importance of reliable recall

INSTRUCTOR #1 & Assistant	INSTRUCTOR # 2 & Assistant
3-Obstacle Left-Turn Sequence • Explain/demo method • Last two obstacles only, I time each dog • Entire 3-obstacle sequence, 2 times each dog	**3-Obstacle Left-Turn Sequence** • Explain/demo method • Last two obstacles only, I time each dog • Entire 3-obstacle sequence, 2 times each dog
3-Obstacle Left-Turn Sequence • Explain/demo method • Last two obstacles only, I time each dog • Entire 3-obstacle sequence, 2 times each dog	**3-Obstacle Left-Turn Sequence** • Explain/demo method • Last two obstacles only, I time each dog • Entire 3-obstacle sequence, 2 times each dog
3-Obstacle Left-Turn Sequence • Explain/demo method • Last two obstacles only, I time each dog • Entire 3-obstacle sequence, 2 times each dog	**3-Obstacle Left-Turn Sequence** • Explain/demo method • Last two obstacles only, I time each dog • Entire 3-obstacle sequence, 2 times each dog

Sample Lesson Plan

Intermediate I Agility — Week 6

Set-Up

Set up sequences with side-switches as described below on each instructor's side. Space obstacles 18 feet apart. Use as many different obstacles as possible to provide supervised practice. A-frame is at 4-1/2 feet, weave poles are sets of 6 offsets, seesaw is ¾ height. Any obstacles not used in the sequences should be set up and available for practice.

Opening Remarks

- Introduction to side-switches

INSTRUCTOR #1 & Assistant

3-Jump Side-Switch Sequence (from Chapter 5)
- Explain/demo pull-back
- 2 times each dog
- Explain/demo cross-in-front
- 2 times each dog
- Explain/demo cross-behind
- 3 times each dog

4-Obstacle Sequence with Side-Switch at Tunnel (from Chapter 5)
- Explain/demo cross-in-front
- 2 times each dog
- Explain/demo cross-behind
- 2 times each dog

INSTRUCTOR # 2 & Assistant

3-Obstacle Sequence with Side-Switch at Dog Walk (from Chapter 5)
- Explain/demo cross-in-front
- 2 times each dog
- Explain /demo cross-behind
- 2 times each dog

3-Obstacle Sequence with Side-Switch at A-frame (at 4-1/2 feet)
- Explain/demo cross-in-front
- 2 times each dog
- Explain /demo cross-behind
- 2 times each dog

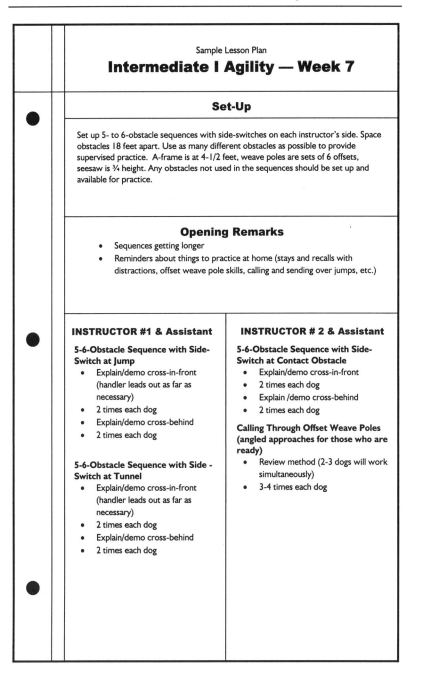

Sample Lesson Plan

Intermediate I Agility — Week 7

Set-Up

Set up 5- to 6-obstacle sequences with side-switches on each instructor's side. Space obstacles 18 feet apart. Use as many different obstacles as possible to provide supervised practice. A-frame is at 4-1/2 feet, weave poles are sets of 6 offsets, seesaw is ¾ height. Any obstacles not used in the sequences should be set up and available for practice.

Opening Remarks

- Sequences getting longer
- Reminders about things to practice at home (stays and recalls with distractions, offset weave pole skills, calling and sending over jumps, etc.)

INSTRUCTOR #1 & Assistant

5-6-Obstacle Sequence with Side-Switch at Jump
- Explain/demo cross-in-front (handler leads out as far as necessary)
- 2 times each dog
- Explain/demo cross-behind
- 2 times each dog

5-6-Obstacle Sequence with Side-Switch at Tunnel
- Explain/demo cross-in-front (handler leads out as far as necessary)
- 2 times each dog
- Explain/demo cross-behind
- 2 times each dog

INSTRUCTOR # 2 & Assistant

5-6-Obstacle Sequence with Side-Switch at Contact Obstacle
- Explain/demo cross-in-front
- 2 times each dog
- Explain /demo cross-behind
- 2 times each dog

Calling Through Offset Weave Poles (angled approaches for those who are ready)
- Review method (2-3 dogs will work simultaneously)
- 3-4 times each dog

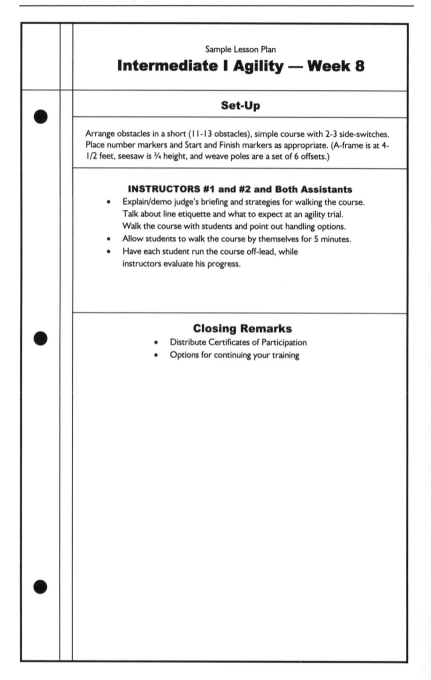

Sample Lesson Plan
Intermediate I Agility — Week 8

Set-Up

Arrange obstacles in a short (11-13 obstacles), simple course with 2-3 side-switches. Place number markers and Start and Finish markers as appropriate. (A-frame is at 4-1/2 feet, seesaw is ¾ height, and weave poles are a set of 6 offsets.)

INSTRUCTORS #1 and #2 and Both Assistants
- Explain/demo judge's briefing and strategies for walking the course. Talk about line etiquette and what to expect at an agility trial. Walk the course with students and point out handling options.
- Allow students to walk the course by themselves for 5 minutes.
- Have each student run the course off-lead, while instructors evaluate his progress.

Closing Remarks
- Distribute Certificates of Participation
- Options for continuing your training

Sample Lesson Plan
Intermediate II Agility — Week 1

Set-Up

SIDE 1	SIDE 2
• *Out!* exercise using two jumps and an open tunnel (from Chapter 6) • Two sets of 12 offset weave poles	• Two 6-7-obstacle sequences with side-switches (A-frame is at 4-3/4 feet, seesaw is ¾ height)

Opening Remarks
- Course goals
- House rules
- Course format (split into two groups – large dogs and small/young dogs)

INSTRUCTOR #1 & Assistant

***Out!* Exercise (from Chapter 6)**
- Explain/demo method
- 3-4 times each dog

12 Offset Weave Poles
- Review skills (parallel distance, getting ahead, pulling away, calling through)
- 3-4 times each dog

INSTRUCTOR # 2 & Assistant

6-7-Obstacle Sequence with Side-Switch
- Explain/demo method
- 2-3 times each dog

6-7-Obstacle Sequence with Side-Switch
- Explain/demo method
- 2-3 times each dog

Sample Lesson Plan
Intermediate II Agility — Week 2

Set-Up

Set up sequences on each instructor's side as described below. Space obstacles 18 feet apart. A-frame is at 5 feet, weave poles are sets of 6 or 12 offsets, seesaw is ¾ height.

Opening Remarks

- More practice with longer sequences and the *Out!* command
- Keep it fun but concentrate on handling

INSTRUCTOR #1 & Assistant

Out! **Exercise (from Chapter 6)**
- Review method
- 3-4 times each dog

6-7-Obstacle Sequence with 2 Side-Switches
- Explain/demo method
- 2-3 times each dog

INSTRUCTOR # 2 & Assistant

6-7-Obstacle Sequence with 2 Side-Switches
- Explain/demo method
- 2-3 times each dog

6-7-Obstacle Sequence with 2 Side-Switches
- Explain/demo method
- 2-3 times each dog

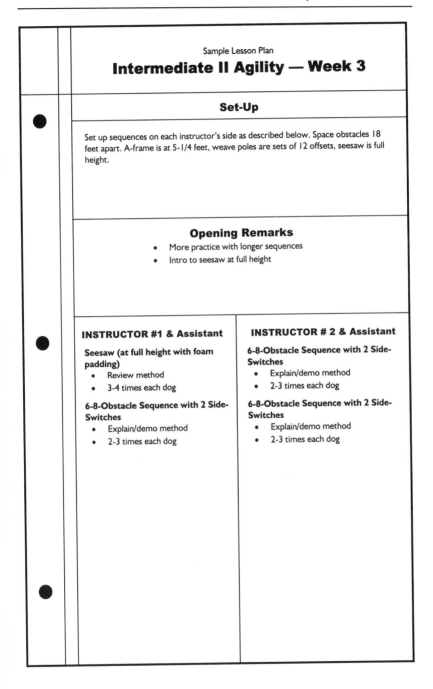

Sample Lesson Plan

Intermediate II Agility — Week 3

Set-Up

Set up sequences on each instructor's side as described below. Space obstacles 18 feet apart. A-frame is at 5-1/4 feet, weave poles are sets of 12 offsets, seesaw is full height.

Opening Remarks

- More practice with longer sequences
- Intro to seesaw at full height

INSTRUCTOR #1 & Assistant	INSTRUCTOR # 2 & Assistant
Seesaw (at full height with foam padding) • Review method • 3-4 times each dog	**6-8-Obstacle Sequence with 2 Side-Switches** • Explain/demo method • 2-3 times each dog
6-8-Obstacle Sequence with 2 Side-Switches • Explain/demo method • 2-3 times each dog	**6-8-Obstacle Sequence with 2 Side-Switches** • Explain/demo method • 2-3 times each dog

Sample Lesson Plan
Intermediate II Agility — Week 4

Set-Up

Set up sequences on each instructor's side as described below. Space obstacles 18 feet apart. A-frame is at 5-1/2 feet, weave poles are sets of 12 offsets, seesaw is full height (5'6").

Opening Remarks

- More practice with longer sequences
- A-frame is now full AKC/NADAC height

INSTRUCTOR #1 & Assistant	INSTRUCTOR # 2 & Assistant
7-8 Obstacle Sequence with 2 Side-Switches • Explain/demo method • 2-3 times each dog	**7-8-Obstacle Sequence with 2 Side-Switches** • Explain/demo method • 2-3 times each dog
7-8-Obstacle Sequence with 2 Side-Switches • Explain/demo method • 2-3 times each dog	**7-8-Obstacle Sequence with 2 Side-Switches** • Explain/demo method • 2-3 times each dog

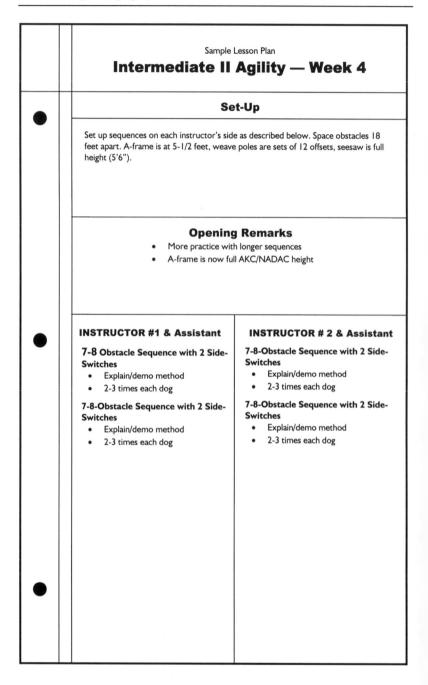

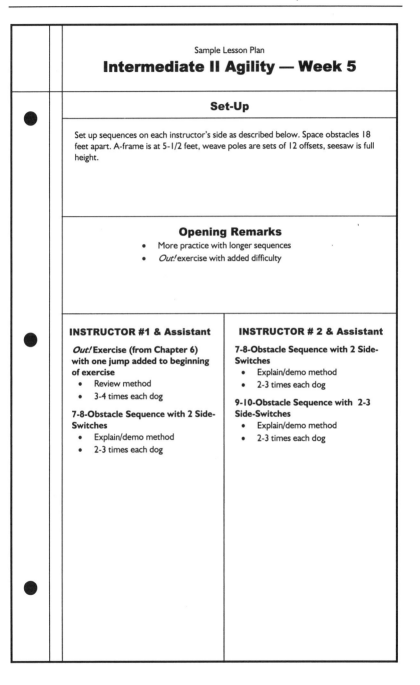

Sample Lesson Plan
Intermediate II Agility — Week 5

Set-Up

Set up sequences on each instructor's side as described below. Space obstacles 18 feet apart. A-frame is at 5-1/2 feet, weave poles are sets of 12 offsets, seesaw is full height.

Opening Remarks

- More practice with longer sequences
- *Out!* exercise with added difficulty

INSTRUCTOR #1 & Assistant	**INSTRUCTOR # 2 & Assistant**
***Out!* Exercise (from Chapter 6) with one jump added to beginning of exercise** • Review method • 3-4 times each dog **7-8-Obstacle Sequence with 2 Side-Switches** • Explain/demo method • 2-3 times each dog	**7-8-Obstacle Sequence with 2 Side-Switches** • Explain/demo method • 2-3 times each dog **9-10-Obstacle Sequence with 2-3 Side-Switches** • Explain/demo method • 2-3 times each dog

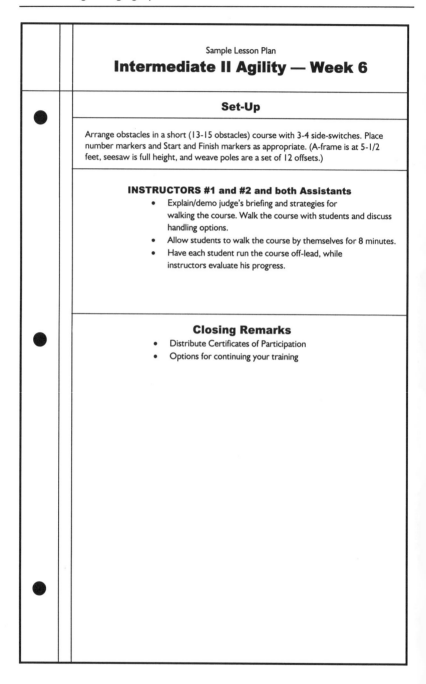

Sample Lesson Plan
Intermediate II Agility — Week 6

Set-Up

Arrange obstacles in a short (13-15 obstacles) course with 3-4 side-switches. Place number markers and Start and Finish markers as appropriate. (A-frame is at 5-1/2 feet, seesaw is full height, and weave poles are a set of 12 offsets.)

INSTRUCTORS #1 and #2 and both Assistants
- Explain/demo judge's briefing and strategies for walking the course. Walk the course with students and discuss handling options.
- Allow students to walk the course by themselves for 8 minutes.
- Have each student run the course off-lead, while instructors evaluate his progress.

Closing Remarks
- Distribute Certificates of Participation
- Options for continuing your training

Appendix B: Video Topic Guide – Tape 2

Below is a listing of topics from the companion video to this book, *Competitive Agility with Jane Simmons-Moake, Tape 2: Sequence Training*. For each topic there is a corresponding number listed to help you quickly find the section of your choice. The number refers to the counter on most video playback units, indicating the time elapsed (hour:minute:second). To use the video topic guide, rewind the tape and press *counter reset* to set the counter to zero. Then fast-forward to the time indicated on the chart.

Obedience commands	3:00
Training for excellence	5:00
Commands	8:33
Signals	10:40
Body language	12:10
Sequence training principles	13:24
Taking advantage of the dog's speed	15:19
Straight-line sequences	16:31
Using training aids	21:23
Call-offs	23:32
Circle exercise	29:19
The *Again!* command	32:45

Turn sequences	35:00
Sequences with contact obstacles	40:18
Side-switches	42:50
On jumps	45:40
On tunnels	50:27
On contacts	51:56
On weave poles	53:42
Building longer sequences	56:35
The *Out!* command	58:28
Distraction training	1:05:20
Putting it all together	1:10:16

What the agility world is saying about the award-winning video series:

Competitive Agility Training
with
Jane Simmons-Moake

"Finally I have found a series of tapes that not only shows every step of the way in getting to the desired goal but demonstrates these steps over and over, until you thoroughly understand how to get there and also the pitfalls to avoid. I can unabashedly recommend the Jane Simmons-Moake Competitive Agility Training tapes to all who have ever considered taking up agility, are currently doing agility or merely want to learn more about it."

"...I have frequently purchased videos that I watched once and then put aside. Not this time! ... I will refer frequently to the beautifully detailed instruction in these tapes."

"...Sequences of actual trials are also included and really helped me to put into reality why particular sequences were so essential to teach."

"...Not only is the content superb, the quality of the tapes is excellent and the filming locale varied... they are a delight to watch."

Helen Phillips, *Front and Finish and Borderlines*

"The videos are so packed with info it would take you a year to do all the exercises and perfect your handling. I think people are insane not to own these videos."

"...THEY ARE SOOO AWESOME. I would highly recommend them to any agility enthusiast."

Angelica E. Steinker, M. Ed.

"Even if you never, ever in your lifetime intend to do competitive Agility training, I still DEMAND that you own this video [Tape 1] if you want to...

♦ Get inside the head of any dog.
♦ Have a dog understand and eagerly respond to your commands.
♦ Have a faster, happier working Obedience dog.
♦ Have a faster, more responsive Schutzund dog.
♦ Have a happier pet and companion."

"...Ms. Moake has written a script loaded with simple, easy-to-understand rationale for both dog and handler."

"...This video shows example after example of excellent trainers and top-working dogs and explains how they get to the high stature in the Agility community. Better yet, it anticipates and shows by several examples the many common mistakes made so that you can nip those mistakes in the bud — before you make them."

Robin Stark, *Rottweiler Quarterly*

"...Without doubt the most comprehensive how-to agility video project on the U.S. market to date..."

Elise Paffrath, *Clean Run Magazine*

"If you want to start getting involved in agility training with your dog or you already are but could use some expert instruction, you cannot do better than to learn from Jane Simmons-Moake, one of the best and most successful agility handlers."

"...This is one of those exceptional productions in which everything is well-done."

"...I would recommend this set of tapes for everyone's agility library."

Gayle George-Sackett, *AKC Gazette*

Competitive Agility Training with Jane Simmons-Moake

This award-winning video series:

- Provides step-by-step instruction from beginning to ultra-advanced agility training.

- Professionally produced by Canine Training Systems, these are tapes you will want to watch again and again.

- Features training demonstrations using 26 breeds, 70 dogs, and 43 handlers.

- Includes both positive and negative examples to illustrate the consequences of handling choices.

Jane's methods:

- Focus on smooth excellence from the start.

- Emphasize skill-building to isolate and train essential dog and handler skills.

- Place early emphasis on distance handling to take advantage of the dog's speed.

- Result in competitive success for people of all ages, shapes, and sizes.

- Are motivational and fun!

Jane Simmons-Moake is one of the world's foremost agility trainers. A top-winning competitor, veteran judge, and award-winning author, Jane runs one of the nation's most successful agility training organizations, FlashPaws Agility Training Center in Houston, Texas. A popular seminar leader in the U.S. and abroad, Jane has also competed internationally as a member of the 1996 and 1997 U.S World Championship Agility Teams.

COMPETITIVE AGILITY TRAINING

with

Jane Simmons-Moake

Bill Newcomb

Named "Best Video Production
of the Year"
by the Dog Writers' Association of America

Tape 1: Obstacle Training

Teach your dog to master each obstacle with competitive excellence in mind. Includes important principles for building a strong foundation for all of your agility training. (80 mins.)

Tape 2: Sequence Training

Discover how to sequence smoothly from one obstacle to the next, to reach your dog's highest potential for speed and accuracy. (78 mins.)

Tape 3: Advanced Skills Training

Learn how to isolate and train many of the skills necessary to compete at the highest levels. (80 mins.)

*Each tape is $59.95 (+ $4.50 U.S. shipping and
handling for up to 3 tapes)
OR save $30 when you order all three! TX orders add 7-1/4% tax.*

_____Tape 1: Obstacle Training
_____Tape 2: Sequence Training
_____Tape 3: Advanced Skills Training

Name _____

Address _____

City _____

State_____   Zip _____

Telephone/Fax_____

Mail check or money order (U.S. funds only) to: FlashPaws,
7714 Rolling Fork Lane, Houston, TX 77040-3432
Visa and MasterCard also accepted

Card #_____ Expiration _____

Name on card _____

*(713) 896-8484 phone/fax, E-mail: info@flashpaws.com
web site: www.flashpaws.com*

For information about seminars, books, videos, and our complete line of supplies for the performance dog:

visit our web site at:
www.flashpaws.com

or contact:
FLASHPAWS
7714 Rolling Fork Lane
Houston, TX 77040-3432
(713) 896-8484

E-mail: info@flashpaws.com